THE FASTEST WAY TO CHANGE YOUR LIFE

3 STEPS TO GETTING **UNSTUCK**
& BECOMING **SPIRITUALLY HEALTHY**

VINCE PIERRI
WITH KRISTEN CAVE

Copyright © 2025 The Bridge Church
All rights reserved.
ISBN: 9798342257930

DEDICATION

This book is dedicated to:

- Those who believe they're beyond the reach of God's love
- Those who think it's too late to write a different story
- Those who are convinced they'll never be able to change

You are not beyond His reach. It's not too late. With His help, you can change.

I hope this book will be your path to a new life with Jesus.

CONTENTS

Chapter 1: Help! I Need To Change...1

KNOW

Before We Get Started..12
Chapter 2: Why Saying "Thank You" Changes Everything.............17
Chapter 3: Why You Keep Crashing..33
Chapter 4: Should I Ask God For Things?....................................47
Chapter 5: One Trip To The Roof..57

GROW

Chapter 6: Fast Food Friendships...71
Chapter 7: How To Make Friends..85
Chapter 8: Don't Get Struck Dead...97

GO

Chapter 9: Batteries Not Included..113
Chapter 10: How To Find Your Calling......................................125
Chapter 11: The Purpose Plop...141

Chapter 12: Now What?..153

The Good News: How To Have A Relationship With Jesus.........165
How To Spend Time With Jesus: A Daily Quiet Time Guide........167
Acknowledgments..171
About the Authors...173

INTRODUCTION

1
Help! I Need To Change

There's nothing worse than **wanting to change**...and being **ready to change**...but not knowing **how to change**.

That was my story.

I grew up in church and believed in God.

While I had lived according to how the Bible says you should live for most of high school, during my junior and senior years things started to change. Sex, random hookups, getting drunk, and pornography all slowly became a normal part of my lifestyle.

This continued on through my early twenties.

I stopped going to church as often, but I still believed. Most of my friends were at least sort of Christian.

Some of them knew how I was living. Some of them didn't.

For the people who did know, I acted like I thought it was fine.

I made up all sorts of reasons to them (and sometimes to myself) why the way I was living was okay.

But here's the thing.

Even though I acted like I was fine with my choices, I wasn't. I wanted to change. And I was secretly trying to change.

I told everyone else what I was doing was fine. But behind the scenes, I was trying everything I could to become a different person.

- I committed and recommitted and recommitted every morning.
- Whatever I did the night before, that would be the last time I did it.
- I would go back to church sometimes.
- I would pray sometimes.
- I would try really, really, really hard...

But whatever commitment I made in the morning had evaporated by that night.

I kept telling myself, "You are a Christian. You shouldn't live this way. You don't need to live this way. And someday, you'll be able to change."

But that day never came.

And the more I felt stuck, the further away I drifted from God and other Christians.

I eventually felt like I had to quit church altogether.

I was a total hypocrite, and hypocrites don't belong in church.

IS THIS YOUR STORY?

If you're stuck in that kind of place today, this book is for you.

Maybe you're reading this and you feel overwhelmed. Trapped. You've tried to get unstuck time and time again, only to find yourself right back where you started...

with the same struggle,

the same fear,

the same vice.

Maybe you're struggling with repeated sin, like losing your temper with your children, gossiping to your friends about your other friends, lying to your spouse, sleeping around, or consuming pornography.

Maybe you're feeling dry spiritually. You feel far from God. You don't feel connected to Him on a personal level. You don't feel a sense of purpose or calling in your life.

Maybe you're having relationship problems. You cannot seem to get along with your spouse or significant other, your adult children, or your aging parents.

Maybe you're struggling with fear about the future, about all that seems to be spiraling out of control in your life.

Or maybe you're dealing with depression, anxiety, or another mental health struggle.

We are all wrestling with something in our lives that we want to change.

And when it comes to wanting change, we don't just want things to change slowly or gradually. We want rapid change. We want our lives to move quickly in a completely different direction.

I believe that sense of urgency is a good thing. That's what this book is all about.

The fastest way to change your life.

WHAT AM I DOING WRONG?

If we're being honest, a lot of us think that believing in Jesus is what should make our desired change happen quickly.

Maybe at one point, you were that person who thought that getting saved* was going to be the thing that caused you to transform.

(*If you've never made the decision to give your life to Jesus and you want to make that decision right now, turn to page 165.)

You heard that you are a sinner in need of forgiveness, and because of what Jesus did on the cross, that forgiveness is available. And if you confess with your mouth that Jesus Christ is Lord, you will be saved. Your sins will be forgiven, the Holy Spirit will enter your heart, and you will go to heaven when you die.

All of that is 100% true.

However, a lot of us are thinking, "Okay, I know that. I believe that. But now what? I do believe I'm saved by grace, but I'm not changing. I still feel stuck, and I need my life to change...fast."

Maybe you've also tried some other things to get your life to change, but those things didn't work.

You went to church consistently six weeks in a row, but nothing changed.

You joined a small group, but nothing changed.

You read a book on spiritual growth, but, again, nothing changed.

No matter what you try, nothing is making a difference. So what are you supposed to do to experience the life change you're looking for?

If that's the question you're asking today, then you've come to the right place.

This book is all about the fastest way to change your life.

And I have seen it again and again, change *can* come quickly. But a lot of people never actually find out how to change.

Let me tell you why that is.

THE SOLUTION MAY BE SURPRISING

In most situations in life, the problem and the solution are obviously connected.

But the start of my life changing was realizing this: when it comes to spiritual growth...there isn't always an obvious connection between the problem and solution.

I learned this from a friend and mentor of mine named Ted.

When Ted and I first became friends, Ted started teaching me things.

Different things.

Different practices.

Different disciplines.

Different ways of doing life.

Things I hadn't grown up hearing about in church.

On the surface, these things didn't seem to have anything to do with getting out of the junk I was stuck in.

I saw my problems as a nail, and I was looking for a hammer.

I saw my struggles as an "E" light, and I needed gas in the tank.

But Ted showed me that's not actually how it works.

I learned that when it comes to spiritual transformation, the solution to our problem of lack of personal growth is not what you might expect.

The solution may be surprising.

Years ago, when I was still single, I went to work out at the gym to do some cardio. I had gotten into decent shape at this point, and around the same time, there was a friend of a friend who was also trying to get in shape. One day, she asked me to share my workout routine with her, and we ended up going to the gym together. (I was not at all qualified to be a personal trainer, but that's just how it happened.)

So we're at the gym, and we start out on the elliptical. After spending about five minutes on the elliptical, she starts going, "Oh my goodness, I'm in so much pain. I've got a cramp in my side, and it hurts so bad. I don't think I can keep going."

It seemed very odd to me at first that she was having trouble because we weren't going super fast, we hadn't been going that long, and she wasn't really out of shape. So it was confusing to me as to why she was in so much pain so quickly.

I'm not a doctor by any means, but something in my gut told me to ask her what she'd had to drink that day. When I asked her that question, she told me that all she'd had to drink all day was Mountain Dew...and it was lunchtime.

No wonder she was in pain! She was **completely** dehydrated.

But don't miss this. She didn't *feel* dehydrated. Why? Because she had just drank a bottle of Mountain Dew.

I handed her a water bottle and told her to drink half of it right then and there. She chugged the water, and then looked at me with a surprised expression on her face, "The pain is gone," she said. "My side cramp disappeared!"

Now don't miss this.

She didn't feel dehydrated, but she was.

When she felt the pain of the side cramp, she didn't think, "solution = water bottle." And yet, that's what the reality was. She was dehydrated, even though she couldn't see that on her own. The solution was to drink water, and when she drank water, she immediately felt better.

The situation changed fast, but the solution was unexpected.

All it took was gaining the knowledge of what was really going wrong and how to fix it.

This same principle is true when it comes to our spiritual lives.

We misunderstand what's causing our problems.

And as a result, we can't find the right solutions.

We use hammers on screws. We put diesel instead of regular gas in the tank.

But when we identify the problems and solutions correctly, there can be very quick change that takes place.

This book is about learning how to drink water spiritually.

It's about learning to identify the pain and struggle and stuckness in your life as spiritual dehydration.

It's about taking steps to become spiritually healthy in ways that may seem unexpected.

Let's take that image of health one step further.

UNDERSTANDING HOW YOU'RE WIRED (SPIRITUALLY)

When it comes to physical health, you are wired to need three things.

1. Eating healthy foods

2. Drinking enough water

3. Exercising (even just a little)

No matter what else might be going right or wrong in your health, you will never feel good and strong without food, water, and some very basic exercise.

In fact, if you're doing none of the three, you are going to feel horrible no matter what else might be going on physically.

But if you start eating decently, drinking water, and even taking a few walks a week, you will start to see a very rapid change in your physical well-being.

The premise of this book is that in the same way every human being is wired to need healthy food, drink enough water, and do enough exercise to be physically healthy, there are three things every human being needs to do to be **spiritually healthy**.

If you haven't been doing the three activities this book is centered around, you're not going to be spiritually healthy...

...and change will not happen in your life.

But as you start to do the three activities, you WILL become spiritually healthy, and change WILL come quickly.

The picture of what I've learned about spiritual growth is this.

Just as humans need food, water, and exercise, Christians need to:

1. KNOW
2. GROW
3. GO

That's what this book is all about.

KNOWING, GROWING, and GOING.

These three concepts are the core of what I learned from that mentor, Ted.

I also discovered over the years that these three concepts are guiding principles throughout Scripture.

Now that I am a pastor, they are the three fundamentals we have built our church on.

I cannot wait to share with you these three foundational principles that have not only changed my life but also the lives of countless others.

We've devoted a section of this book to each principle.

Some of you may discover you've already been doing some of what we'll talk about. But if you aren't doing all three, KNOWING, GROWING, and GOING, I am not surprised that you're feeling stuck.

Just as you were designed for food, water, and exercise, and you can't have physical health without them, you were designed to KNOW, GROW, and GO, and you can't be spiritually healthy without all three.

If you're looking for the fastest way to change your life, KNOWING, GROWING, and GOING is your answer.

As soon as you start doing all of these three things, you're going to notice a big change in a short amount of time.

WHAT DOES IT MEAN TO KNOW, GROW, AND GO?

I hope by this point you're wondering what those three words mean. That's what we'll discover for the rest of this book.

I'm trying to keep a little suspense on purpose here so you actually read the thing!

But what I can tell you is that if you learn to understand and apply what it means to KNOW, GROW, and GO, you're not going to feel so stuck anymore.

You're going to feel closer to God and develop a deep, meaningful relationship with Him.

You're going to find the strength and power you need to overcome the struggles you've been battling for years.

You're going to find freedom from the sin you've been entangled in for far too long.

You're going to find purpose in this life and begin to make a difference in the world around you.

And that's just the beginning, my friend.

God has a big plan for your life. And if you're ready to start living out that plan, you have to start KNOWING, GROWING, and GOING.

MY HOPE FOR YOU

The entire goal of this book is to inspire you to take these three steps: KNOW, GROW, and GO.

But let me be honest.

This will not be easy.

If you're not eating healthy, staying hydrated, or exercising, adopting those three things would be a big change, wouldn't it?

In the same way, KNOWING, GROWING, and GOING will be a big change.

I would give you something easier if I believed that something easier would work.

But just like healthy food, water, and physical activity is the fastest way to feel better physically, KNOWING, GROWING, and GOING is the fastest way to start doing better spiritually.

After 15 years of living this out, 10 years of ministry, and five years of being a lead pastor, I wholeheartedly believe that doing these three things is the fastest way to change your life.

So let's begin with KNOW and what that first step is all about.

KNOW

BEFORE WE GET STARTED

The first part of the journey of following Jesus involves your personal relationship with God. This is what we're going to refer to as "KNOW."

KNOWING God means developing a deep, personal relationship with Him.

Now, don't get me wrong. Many of us have been told that a personal relationship with God is ALL that we need for our lives to change. Though this is step one, you'll need steps two and three as well. But you also can't miss the KNOW part either.

You can't skip step one.

Typically, when I talk to people about KNOWING God and having a personal relationship with Him, I usually refer to these three basic practices:

1. Church attendance
2. Prayer
3. Bible reading

In this section of the book on KNOWING God, we're going to be focusing specifically on prayer and how you can come to know God more deeply through communication with Him.

That being said, I want to give you a little context as to how this part of the book is formatted. Each chapter is going to correspond with the acronym P.R.A.Y. Here's what that acronym stands for:

- **P**raise (thanking God for His blessings)
- **R**epent (turning your back on your sin)
- **A**sk (talking to God about your wants and needs)
- **Y**ield (surrendering your heart to God's plan)

I didn't come up with the acronym. No one's sure where it originated, but countless Christians have found it incredibly helpful.

Let me break it down even further.

The first chapter in this section will talk about the importance of practicing gratitude (or **praising** God) when you pray and how gratitude strengthens your relationship with Him.

The second chapter will talk about how **repenting** helps us maintain a pure heart before God. We'll learn why this is so important because what happens in our hearts ultimately happens in our lives.

The third chapter will talk about why **asking** God for things isn't a bad thing but is actually pivotal in establishing a strong relationship with Him.

And finally, the fourth chapter in this section will talk about how much God can do when we are **yielding** to Him and intentionally carving out time to pray to Him each day.

Now, all that being said, I want to clarify why we're only talking about prayer and why we aren't talking about church attendance and Bible reading in this section:

1. To give prayer its due diligence, we cut the content on telling you to go to church. One reason for that is that you're likely already attending church if you're reading this book. And if you're not, it's fairly simple to get started...**just show up.**

2. The reason why we're not deep-diving into why and how to read the Bible is that we've already developed a separate and free resource you can download on that topic.

    You can visit https://www.thebridgenky.com/discover-the-bible and download a free resource I wrote called "The Greatest Story Ever Told." This booklet is a step-by-step guide to the Bible that helps you navigate and understand the structure and timeline of the Word of God. You can also check out the entire sermon series I preached to go along with this booklet by visiting the same link.

Now, I'm not going to keep you waiting any longer. Let's dive into what it looks like to KNOW God, specifically through prayer.

"Daring to utter a prayer of nothing but "Thank you, God" is to light a kindling in your relationship with Him that will transform who you realize God is and how much you need Him like the very air you breathe." — Ben Moore

2

Why Saying "Thank You" Changes Everything

If you want your life to change, you have to step into a deeper personal relationship with God.

And central to knowing God better is this:

Learning to say thank you.

It's expressing gratitude to Him. It's thanking Him for His work in your life. It's worshiping Him and praising Him for His goodness.

It might not seem like much at first. But practicing gratitude is the first BIG step in KNOWING God, and it's the first big step in your life changing.

This is the "P" of our prayer acronym.

For some people, the fact that God wants us to praise Him makes God seem like a first-class egomaniac. I wish we could fully dive into why God asks us to worship Him, but that would be another book entirely.

For now, I want you to know that gratitude is not just for God's benefit.

It's for ours too.

If we want our lives to change, if we want to become spiritually healthier, we have to understand the surprising truth that gratitude is actually crucial.

GRATITUDE IS NO SMALL MATTER

When you were little and someone would give you something, whether it was a birthday gift, a compliment, or an extra helping of mashed potatoes at Thanksgiving, what would your parents say to you?

"Say thank you!"

We probably heard our parents make that statement thousands of times growing up. We could barely move on to the next gift or the next side dish in the buffet line without being told to be grateful for whatever we'd just been given.

And at that time, saying thank you felt anything but life-changing. It was basically just annoying. It felt obligatory and polite, a necessary evil to get along in adult society.

This mindset about gratitude travels with most of us long after we graduate from childhood, particularly when it comes to our relationship with God.

We know we're supposed to thank God. We know we're supposed to worship Him and praise Him.

But when we do it, we do it because we feel like we're supposed to.

Therefore, most of us don't express gratitude that often.

And when we do take the time to praise God, we only express gratitude for the big things.

We thank Him that the fender bender we got into on our way to work wasn't a more serious or fatal crash.

We thank Him that a tree didn't fall on our house during the big storm.

Or we thank Him that the test results came back negative for cancer.

What I want to show you is that when you make gratitude, praise, and thanksgiving towards God a regular practice – even if it's just for the simple, mundane things – it will radically change your life.

To show you what I'm talking about, let's look at a story from the Book of Acts.

GREATER GRATITUDE = GREATER GRIT

In case you're not familiar, the Book of Acts tells the story of everything that happened to the early Christians after Jesus was resurrected and went back to heaven. This book covers many of the trials and triumphs the early church endured.

In Acts 5, there was a group of Jesus followers, also called apostles, who were arrested for preaching the good news of Jesus. (You'll see that this happens quite often as you keep reading this book.)

In the middle of the night, while they were in prison, an angel appeared to the apostles, opened the jail doors, and instructed them to go to the temple courts and keep teaching people about Jesus.

The apostles obeyed and went back to preaching but were once again reprimanded. This time the consequence wasn't jail, but a brutal torture with whips in public. After the flogging, they were released and given a second warning to stop talking about Jesus.

Now, to be honest, if the apostles had started complaining, or getting discouraged, or even having angry outbursts towards God, I wouldn't have blamed them. It would make complete sense. Here they were, spending all of their time, energy, and resources trying to do the right thing - trying to tell more people about Jesus. And what did they get in return?

Suffering.

I'd say a little anger or frustration would have been understandable, warranted even.

But that's not how the apostles responded. They chose a different path. Let's look at exactly what happened after the apostles faced their punishment.

"The apostles left the Sanhedrin [after being flogged], rejoicing because they had been counted worthy of suffering disgrace for the Name [of Jesus]" (Acts 5:41).

The apostles **rejoiced.**

They praised.

They worshiped.

They thanked God in the midst of their suffering and mistreatment.

Rather than drowning in self-pity, depression, or discouragement, they responded by praising God and thanking Him for the goodness they could see in their situation.

This decision to be grateful resulted in them experiencing a fresh boldness and readiness for the path ahead. The very next sentence tells us,

"Day after day, in the temple courts and from house to house, they never stopped teaching and proclaiming the good news that Jesus is the Messiah" (Acts 5:42).

What gave the disciples the strength to keep on moving? To find new strength? To endure the trial ahead of them?

I'll tell you what. It was the simple act of expressing gratitude in the midst of hardship.

This story demonstrates a simple principle we see all across the Book of Acts.

The more we give thanks to God, the more we receive strength from God.

Let me say it again for the people in the back.

The more we give thanks to God, the more we receive strength from God.

As we express gratitude to God, *especially* in the midst of hardship, trial, difficulty, and tragedy, God strengthens and reforms our hearts. Gratitude trains our hearts to focus on the goodness of God. The more we focus on His goodness, grace, and provision, the more we find the strength to face the difficulties ahead.

And trust me, you're going to need strength.

So much of being stuck comes from a lack of strength.

You're going to need strength to gain victory over the addiction.

You're going to need strength to improve your marriage.

You're going to need strength to overcome your anger problem, your lustful thoughts, your parenting struggles, your depression, and your anxiety.

You're going to need strength to find your purpose and live out your calling.

The fastest way to change your life starts with fostering an attitude of gratitude.

So if you want that kind of life-changing strength, you're going to have to start with practicing gratitude.

A SNAPSHOT OF MY GRATITUDE JOURNEY

A few years back when I first became the lead pastor at The Bridge, I was having a really hard time. It was my first year being a lead pastor, and if I'm being honest, I didn't really know what I was doing. So not only was I having a hard time getting used to being a pastor, but the people at the church were having a hard time getting used to me being their pastor.

On top of that, I had stepped into the role after a sudden and difficult transition from our founding pastor. Besides that, we were in the middle of COVID-19, a highly tense presidential election, and racial unrest across the country.

I remember the first few weeks I preached, I found myself getting a little cocky when I walked out into the lobby and saw a bunch of people crying. I thought to myself, "Wow! I must have preached quite a message if this many people are moved to the point of tears!"

But it turns out that that's not why they were crying at all! They were crying because I was their pastor now, and they were anything but thrilled about it. Talk about a humbling moment for Pastor Vince.

I had gotten some good advice to not make any big changes in the first year of leadership. And I followed that advice as best I could. But it seemed like nothing was working. I'm sure a lot of the angst was my own fault, but it seemed like everyone was mad at me. There were constant angry emails, angry phone calls, and angry meetings. People were leaving. Some were even recruiting whole teams of people to leave with them. 80% of the staff quit or were fired in the first year or two. There were many long Facebook posts about what a horrible pastor I was. And the posts were often coupled with endless comments of people agreeing.

Honestly, I was very depressed. I felt like I was a failure. I was letting everyone down. Nothing was ever going to change or get better.

And then I started to doubt. Maybe I had picked the wrong calling. Or maybe I heard God wrong. Or maybe God was mad at me and punishing me for something.

What if I had absolutely blown it and there was no way out? What if I was going to be stuck like this forever?

Quitting didn't feel right, because leaving felt like disobedience. But staying also felt like failure.

Needless to say, I was not doing well.

In the midst of all this chaos, I called my pastor friend and mentor Dave. I filled him in on the entire sob story, not leaving out a single detail. Once I finished ranting and finally gave Dave some space to respond, he said,

"Vince, you need to start practicing some gratitude in your life."

I sat silently in disbelief at his response. Did he not just hear how awful my life is right now?

But Dave persisted.

"You need to practice gratitude, Vince. You need to thank God for all the blessings He's given you."

If anyone else had said that to me in that moment, I would have been completely annoyed. I would have written them off as being too churchy and moved on to someone else, convinced there was a deeper solution to all of my problems.

But because it was Dave, and I trusted Dave with everything in me, I did what he said.

Every morning, when I would spend time with God, I would practice gratitude and thank God for the things He'd given me. Sometimes the list of things to be grateful for felt fairly short, but I persisted anyway. I thanked Him for my wife, my health, my job, the baptisms that were happening in the church. I even tried to thank Him for giving me this role as the pastor of The Bridge, regardless of how hard it was at the time.

And over time, I started to notice a difference in how I viewed life and how I viewed God.

I thought of more and more blessings God had given me that I had taken for granted like my friends, mentors, a roof over my head, gas in the tank, food on the table, and the list kept going. All of my daily needs that I had taken for granted started to feel like sure signs of God's love and care for me.

I started to see the frustration fade.

I started to feel strengthened to face the tough circumstances I found myself in.

And it all started with practicing a little gratitude.

The same can be true for you, friend. Gratitude really does make a difference. I've seen it happen in my own life, and I know for a fact it can happen in your life as well.

Remember, the more you give thanks to God, the more you'll receive strength from God.

When you thank God *in the midst* of your job stress, you'll find strength for your job stress.

When you thank God *in the midst* of your loneliness, you'll find strength for your loneliness.

When you thank God *in the midst* of your depression, you'll find strength for your depression.

When you thank God *in the midst* of your anxiety, you'll find strength for your anxiety.

When you thank God *in the midst* of your lack of direction, you'll find strength for your lack of direction.

You get the idea.

Now, let's deep dive this a little more.

I believe there are three specific changes gratitude brings when we practice it.

1. GRATITUDE GIVES OUR MINDS MOMENTUM

At the time we are working on this book, I recently preached a sermon where I told a story about my love for McDonald's double cheeseburgers.

When I was in the midst of writing the sermon, I hadn't had a McDonald's double cheeseburger in a long time. I love them so much, and we always get them when my wife and I go on road trips, but it had been a minute since I'd been able to enjoy a double cheeseburger.

But as I continued working on the sermon, and then practiced the sermon, and then preached the sermon twice on Sunday morning, and then talked to a surprising amount of people in the lobby afterward about our mutual love for McDonald's double cheeseburgers, all I could think about was how badly I wanted to eat a McDonald's double cheeseburger.

The next few weeks after preaching that sermon, I went to McDonald's three to four times when I normally go only a few times a year.

Why did that happen? Because **our minds have momentum.**

When we are constantly thinking about something and talking about something, our minds, words, and actions continue in that direction. The momentum snowballs.

Just like this worked with my love for McDonald's double cheeseburgers, it works the same way with gratitude.

If you direct your mind toward gratitude for God's love, your mind will move in that direction and away from fear of condemnation.

If you direct your mind toward gratitude for God's provision, your mind will move in that direction and away from fear for the future.

If you direct your mind toward gratitude for God's presence, your mind will move in that direction and away from fear of isolation.

Gratitude gives us the momentum we need to go in a better direction.

(Also, if you're thinking about McDonald's now, I apologize.)

2. GRATITUDE SOFTENS OUR HEARTS

My wife Joanna and I used to watch a show called "Blown Away," which is a glass-blowing competition show. We watched all three seasons of this show, including the Christmas special.

I know, I know. How cool are we?

It was absolutely fascinating to watch these people form all of these incredible creations by blowing glass.

One detail the glass blowers would share often throughout the show is how hot the oven was. In order to get the glass into a soft, moldable state, the artists would put the glass in a 2000-degree oven.

Once the glass was hot enough, they would pull the glass out of the oven and begin to form it into some sort of creation like a vase or a Christmas ornament.

At some point in the forming process, the glass would get too cool to where it couldn't be molded anymore. So they would stick the glass back in the fire to heat it up so that it would become malleable again. This process would be repeated as many times as necessary.

Part of why we loved the show is because there is nothing cooler than hot, glowing glass. Simply mesmerizing.

Our hearts are kind of like glass in the hands of an expert glass blower.

Gratitude is kind of like the fire that softens our hearts to be formed and molded into a better state.

If you don't like the state of your heart surrounding your job, your marriage, your relationship with your kids, your singleness, your living situation, etc., gratitude is the fire we can use to soften our hearts when it comes to these difficulties we're facing.

If we want to have a deep, meaningful, transformational relationship with God, our hearts need to be soft toward Him. Gratitude brings us to a place of openness where we can receive direction, correction, and encouragement from God.

God loves when our hearts are warm, soft, and moldable. He actually loves seeing that way more than I loved seeing the glass on the TV show.

Our hearts can change surrounding our circumstances, but that change must start with gratitude.

3. GRATITUDE LEADS TO DEEPER RELATIONSHIP

Any relationship that lacks gratitude is going to lack intimacy. There's no way around it.

Whether it's in a marriage relationship, a parent/child relationship, or a boss/employee relationship, we always move toward people who express more gratitude than less.

And typically, the more a relationship matures, the more gratitude is present.

There's an old saying that goes, "Parents get a lot smarter once their kids turn 18." If you're a parent of adult children, then you've probably experienced this, and you also might be chuckling to yourself right about now. As your kids mature, they start to gain a better understanding of all the things you did for them and all the reasons why you did the things you did as a parent.

Obviously, no parent is perfect, but it is a pretty neat thing to see a kid express more gratitude for the hard work their parents put into raising them once the kid matures and their relationship with their parent matures.

Our relationship with God works the same way. As you express gratitude, God responds in the same way people naturally do - He moves toward us and our relationship with Him matures. It grows deeper. It thrives.

Now, God does love you unconditionally. And you can't earn His love. But when we seek Him, we come to know Him more deeply, and one of the ways we seek Him is through gratitude.

GRATITUDE WORKS IN THE DEEPEST DARKNESS

Gratitude is not just what gets us through a long stressful day at work, or the missed credit card payment, or the child that won't stop crying. Gratitude is what gave the disciples strength to keep preaching after they were beaten. And gratitude is what gives us the strength to keep going even in the most difficult seasons of life.

This reality reminds me of my friend Gina.

Gina was a long-time attender of our church, The Bridge, and she loved the Lord with everything in her. And not only did she love God, but she loved people really well.

There were so many Sunday mornings my day was brightened when Gina would say hello to me from the church cafe, which she used to run. I'm convinced that the people who stuck around at our church after the founding pastor retired stayed because they went to the cafe and met Gina. She made up for a lot of my bad sermons and poor leadership decisions.

She was a wonderful woman. She radiated the love of Jesus. She was the mom everyone wished they had.

A couple of years back, Gina received a heart-breaking cancer diagnosis. By the time they caught the cancer, it was already stage four, and the doctors weren't sure how much they were going to be able to do to help her.

A couple of days after she received the news, my wife and I went to visit Gina. To be honest, I was very anxious. I was still very new to this pastoring thing at the time. I had no idea how I was going to minister to someone who was walking through such difficult circumstances. I had never sat with anyone right after they had been diagnosed with terminal cancer. So needless to say, I was a big ball of nerves on my way to Gina's house.

To try to prepare myself for this visit, I called Gina's daughter Emily, who was our Kids Ministry Director at the time. I asked Emily how Gina was doing, and Emily was very reassuring.

"She's honestly doing great," Emily said, "She's feeling very hopeful and optimistic, which has been so encouraging to see!"

I remember being amazed by Emily's response, but I also remember thinking, "Gina must be absolutely in denial."

Surely the reality of her situation hadn't sunk in, and she was holding onto some sort of blind optimism in the midst of this heartbreaking diagnosis.

So in light of all this, I mentally prepared myself to try to love on someone who just wasn't yet living in reality.

But as my wife and I walked into Gina's house and sat down next to her, I think I said two words before Gina started preaching to us.

She went on and on about the goodness and faithfulness of God.

"God is just so loving," she said with the most genuine smile on her face. "I have no doubt He's going to use this for good. I believe with all my heart that I'm going to be healed. And I know He's going to use this experience to help other people see that God is a healer and that He is good!"

At this point, I'm thinking that this is where the denial comes in because she's convinced she's going to be healed.

Now, don't get me wrong. I knew that healing was definitely a possibility! After all, we serve a big God and I have seen some incredible miracles. However, this situation wasn't looking very promising, and I thought at first that Gina just wasn't facing her reality. But she wasn't done.

"But even if I don't get healed," she said, still smiling, "that just means I get to go home and be with Jesus early." She was just as genuine saying she was excited to meet Jesus sooner than she had planned as she was saying she believed she was going to be healed.

Then she started going on and on about how we needed to do whatever we could to help other people meet Jesus because life is short and eternity is real.

I was amazed as I listened to Gina speak on and on about the goodness of God in her life.

She was not in denial.

She was in love with Jesus.

She did not see herself as a victim but as a beloved daughter waiting for an eternal inheritance.

In the midst of a terminal cancer diagnosis, all Gina felt was thanksgiving and joy.

I was witnessing the effect of a lifetime of practicing gratitude.

She had become an unstoppable force of love and goodness in the world.

And Gina lived the rest of her days overflowing with that same gratitude until she passed away two years after her diagnosis. During those two years, her confidence never wavered. Countless people's faith was built or rebuilt watching Gina live a life of gratitude even as her days on planet Earth were winding down.

Though I did not at all feel worthy of this, I ended up having the great honor of being the pastor at Gina's funeral. She had demanded that we do a full-on old-school altar call (which I normally don't do at funerals). But of course, we honored her request, and several people gave their lives to Jesus that afternoon.

It was a beautiful thing.

I tell you this story to make sure you understand how powerful gratitude can be. Gratitude is strong enough to give you the strength you need to endure cancer, job loss, divorce, or even losing a child.

Like I said at the beginning of this chapter, it might seem trivial at first glance, and it might have not seemed like a big deal when you opened that birthday present when you were five years old, but I promise you, saying "thank you" really can change everything.

"Spending time praying and reading my Bible has changed my life. I went from living a life of being lost in sin and shame to a life of desiring to honor God in everything I do and say. Before, I lived for myself, and now I live to honor the Holy King." - Tracie Johnson

3
Why You Keep Crashing

A few years ago, my wife and I took a vacation to South Carolina. I am the most boring vacationer in the world and was secretly hoping that my wife would also want to sit inside the Airbnb all day. But since she is a normal person, she talked me into going to the beach with her.

Once we got to the beach, the South Carolina heat showed us no mercy and we were already dripping sweat when we settled into our beach chairs. It wasn't long before we decided to get in the water to cool off.

If you've ever been in the ocean before, then you know as the waves come in, you have to jump with them so they don't crash over you and swallow you up. So every single time a wave would come toward us, Joanna and I would jump with the wave. My inner boring old man eventually surrendered, and we started having a good time. Forty-five minutes or so flew by.

Eventually, we decided to head back to our chairs. But when I turned around to face the shore, I panicked. "Where are our beach chairs?" I shouted, very confused. "Jo, I think someone stole our beach chairs!"

Despite my paranoia that we had been robbed, I quickly realized that our beach chairs hadn't been touched. We had just drifted because the wave jumping had slowly pulled us away from where we started. We had traveled down the shoreline so far that the beach chairs were no longer in our sight. Left on the autopilot of our ocean frolicking, we had drifted quite a distance from our original location.

Do you know why it's so hard for us to change? Do you know why we often keep going backward?

Because the forces of life pulling your heart away from God are far stronger than the Atlantic Ocean.

SPIRITUAL DRIFTING

As we splash through our days, countless little waves are pulling us further and further from the shoreline of walking with Jesus.

The disappointment of not completing a goal is a little wave that pulls us toward doubt.

The criticism of our spouse is a little wave that pulls us toward resentment.

The constant negative Nelly news cycle is a series of little waves pulling us toward fear.

Our social media feed is an endless barrage of waves that pull us toward insecurity, greed, and lust.

And most of us just drift merrily along, going about our days, with no system to check if we're being pulled away from our original location.

We started out in the right place with the best intentions, thinking, "I want to be a good parent, a good spouse, a good friend…" or "I want to leave the addiction behind, the greed behind, the selfishness behind, the worry behind, the pride behind." We went to church. We maybe even joined a group or started serving in church thinking that would be enough.

But we never created a discipline to see if those intentions were still in place or if the waves of life had pulled us away.

In the same way Jo and I were drifting away on autopilot, our hearts are often drifting away on autopilot as well.

And before we know it, our hearts are as far from Jesus as I was from the beach chairs that day in South Carolina.

The truth is, no Christian can leave their heart on autopilot and not suffer.

This is the way human beings have been since the beginning of the story of the church.

Let's look at just one example from the Book of Acts.

SIMON'S DRIFT

In Acts 8, we meet a man by the name of Simon the Sorcerer. As you can tell by his name, he was a man who was practicing sorcery and witchcraft (aka he was not following Jesus). Because of all of the mind-blowing acts Simon was performing, he was getting a lot of attention in his community.

But around the time Simon is becoming popular, a man named Philip steps onto the scene. Philip is a man of God who shows up to preach about Jesus. Miracles start happening because the power of God is at work through Philip. And as a result, Simon the Sorcerer decides to leave his wands and potions behind and follow Jesus.

Not only that, but Simon the Sorcerer started doing ministry with Philip. He didn't just start showing up to church once a week. He got plugged in and started with the best of intentions.

While Simon did KNOW God as his Savior (in a way), he left his heart on autopilot. He was not practicing the kind of self-examination and direction-changing prayer that we're going to talk about in just a minute.

And the waves of life ended up causing him to drift completely away from God. Here's what happens when Peter and John show up to check on Philip and Simon.

When the apostles in Jerusalem heard that Samaria had accepted the word of God, they sent Peter and John to Samaria. When they arrived, they prayed for the new believers there that they might receive the Holy Spirit, because the Holy Spirit had not yet come on any of them; they had simply been baptized in the name of the Lord Jesus. Then Peter and John placed their hands on them, and they received the Holy Spirit. When Simon saw that the Spirit was given at the laying on of the apostles' hands, he **offered them money** and said, "Give me also this ability so that everyone on whom I lay my hands may receive the Holy Spirit" (Acts 8:14-19, emphasis mine).

When Simon the Sorcerer saw Peter and John praying for people to be filled with the Spirit, something ugly in his heart came to the surface. Simon actually approached Peter and John and offered to *pay them* for the power of the Holy Spirit.

Last I checked, I don't think the Holy Spirit's power is something you can purchase. And Simon knew better. Peter responds to Simon's request with the harshest of rebukes and essentially tells him that he's way off course.

We'd hope that when Peter calls him out, Simon would have changed. But from what we know according to church history, Simon the Sorcerer ended up becoming a false teacher of Christian heresy. He didn't stay with Philip. He didn't repent of his wickedness and selfishness. He didn't make the effort to examine his heart. His life never fully changed.

And that unawareness, that forsaken opportunity to learn to lead his own heart, ended up destroying Simon's life and legacy.

THIS DOESN'T NEED TO BE YOUR STORY ANYMORE

Even though Simon originally walked with the apostles, saw the miracles, and was a part of the action, he left his heart on autopilot, and he ended in a crash.

The same thing is happening to us every day.

You've seen it before.

People come to church, raise their hands during a salvation moment, and with tear-filled eyes, they give their life to Jesus. Then they start coming to church every single week. They start serving. They join a group. Everything looks great on the outside.

But then out of nowhere, we find ourselves saying:

"Wait...that person quit church?"

"Wait...that person had an affair?"

"Wait...that person fell back into that addiction?"

"Wait...that person stopped believing in God altogether?"

Everything can look great on the outside, and then all of a sudden, everything falls apart.

Why? Because that person did not bring their heart to God on a regular basis for examination and purification. In other words, they didn't regularly ask God to take a close look at what was going on inside their hearts so He could help them heal and find freedom from whatever they were struggling with.

Maybe that's your story. If so, know that you're not alone and God has not given up on you. He still loves you just as much as ever.

But...it is time to get our hearts off of autopilot and quit crashing!

The fastest way to change your life requires learning to stop the drift.

How do we do it? Well, you may not like the answer.

TURNING OFF AUTOPILOT

I am fully convinced that **if I do not regularly <u>examine</u> and <u>clean out</u> my heart, it will drift away from God.**

Maybe not right away. Or tomorrow. Or next week or next year. But sooner or later, I will ruin my life.

I've got to make it a practice to be honest with myself, confess my sin, and ask God to change me.

This is the "R" of our P.R.A.Y. acronym, and it stands for **repentance**. Repentance simply means turning thoughts and actions over to God. It is an act that begins with self-examination and ends with a change of direction.

If I don't regularly examine my heart, my marriage will not be strong, my finances will not be stable, my leadership will be weak or manipulative, my eyes will be lustful, and my hope will be slowly dimming. I must *regularly* bring my heart to God and let him fix whatever has most recently broken or started to get sick inside of me.

If I let unhealthy patterns continue, I fully believe I will destroy my marriage, my finances, my leadership, and my witness.

I know this motivation to spend time with God may feel heavy and fear-driven, but the dangers of not doing it are very real.

Today, I want to give you one simple tool to examine and lead your heart back to health, a tool that is ultimately all about repentance.

It is called digging a layer deeper.

SEEING PAST THE SURFACE

Right now, we are in a major renovation project at our church. Part of that project involves getting a completely new parking lot.

As I'm writing this chapter, our parking lot is cracked and broken with massive potholes. The interesting thing is that these potholes are also often with water even if it hasn't rained in weeks.

The reason for the water is the fact that there are underground streams that destroy our parking lot from the bottom up.

In an attempt to save ourselves the pain of spending hundreds of thousands of dollars, we've been spending around $20,000 each year to resurface the parking lot. A crew comes out and within a day the parking lot looks brand new. There's a fresh layer of blacktop, new painted lines, and a fresh-out-of-the-box shine.

The only problem? We didn't actually dig down deep enough to fix the underlying issue.

And within a few months, the parking lot is right back to where it was. Cracked, broken, and full of holes filled with water from the destructive underground water currents.

This is the same problem that goes wrong when it comes to our hearts. We have trouble getting all the way down to the layers where the strongest currents run that are actually tearing up the surface of our lives.

If we want our lives to change, we need to **dig deeper**.

Let me give you an example of what digging deeper looks like.

We could use any sort of painful or stressful situation, but let's use one that all of us have faced before: dealing with stress at work.

Maybe you're finding yourself feeling super anxious whenever you walk into work. The thought of getting up and going into the office is so overwhelming that it's almost unbearable.

So you ask yourself, why am I so worried?

What comes to the surface is this thought: "I'm worried I won't get promoted at my job."

Now, that's probably 100% true.

But if you stop there, you've only dug down one layer.

You can pray and ask God to help you be less worried about the promotion, but before you know it, the anxiety will be right back. You dealt with the surface-level problem, but you didn't deal with the deep underlying currents.

This same thing can happen in every area of life. We pray about our lives, but when it comes to our own hearts, we are not aware of the deep undercurrents, and they remain unaddressed.

This kind of prayer is a good start.

But you've got to dig deeper and find the deeper streams in your heart.

GETTING TO THE DEEPER LAYERS

This past summer we finally spent the money to dig down a full two feet across the entire parking lot to handle the root issue. There were drainage systems installed to deal with the water currents at a deep level. The process took quite a long time and required a much more significant financial investment.

That's the bad news. But the good news is that the change will last. In fact, the new parking lot came with a 20-year warranty!

The same thing needs to happen in your heart. You have to slow down. Dig down. And ask God to show you all of the different possible underground currents that are tearing up the surface of your life.

Let's go back to our work example.

Identifying the surface-level issue is step one. But that's not where we need to stop. If you stop there, all you've done is put a fresh coat of blacktop on the parking lot of your heart.

You need to ask yourself, "***Why*** am I so worried about not getting promoted? What are the underground currents that I can only identify if I dig down? Is there fear behind the fear? A worry beneath the worry? What are the underground destructive streams?"

This is where you need to get really honest and let God reveal what is actually happening inside you.

This is where things get more painful, but also more real.

Here are some possible destructive underground streams for our work stress example.

Underground Stream 1: I want to get promoted because I grew up in poverty and I'm afraid I won't be able to provide for my family moving forward.

Underground Stream 2: I want to get promoted because I'm still trying to make my parents happy. I never felt like I could do enough to make them proud, so if I get promoted, then surely, they'll be proud of me.

Underground Stream 3: I want to get promoted because I think that will make me attractive to other people. I'm single, and I want to get married. So, if I get the promotion, I'll look more impressive and attractive, therefore more people will want to date me, and it'll make it easier to find my person.

Do you see how much deeper these things are?

And guess what? There might be layers even deeper.

Sometimes you have to dig for a while.

There are countless deep, unseen streams that secretly destroy our minds and actions. They're not always bad in and of themselves. They're often good things taken to the extremes. Here are a few examples:

- The stream of wanting to be liked or desired
- The stream of wanting control
- The stream of wanting freedom
- The stream of wanting financial stability
- The stream of wanting to be comfortable
- The stream of wanting to avoid conflict
- The stream of wanting to feel safe

The practice of examining our hearts may not seem that important.

But if you don't dig down and identify your undercurrents, they will always win.

This is why you can make a decision to follow Jesus in the morning and have already bailed by the night.

You weren't lying to yourself that morning. But you also haven't dealt with the deep heart-level streams pulling you away from Jesus.

The fastest way to change your life requires that you deal with the deepest root issues driving your behaviors.

WHAT DO WE DO ABOUT THOSE CURRENTS?

It can be scary to start digging into our hearts and finding some dirty water flowing deep inside.

It's especially scary because we're not sure what we should even do once we find it.

But here's the good news.

When you can see clearly the issue going wrong, God has a way of giving you the motivation and tools to fix it.

My wife Joanna is a wonderful cook. It's one of the many reasons why I love her (I promise it's not the only reason). There was this one particular evening she made this delicious salmon dish for the two of us. I absolutely loved it. And to my delight, there were leftovers after dinner. So I decided to box them up in some Tupperware for my lunch the following day.

But when the next day came around, I forgot about the salmon.

And then I forgot about it the next day.

And the day after that.

Before I knew it, eight days had passed before I remembered the salmon leftovers were still in the fridge.

So as my stomach growled with lunchtime approaching, I asked Joanna, "Hey, do you think this salmon in the fridge is still good?" She assured me very quickly that there was no way it was still edible, but I decided to check things out for myself.

I pulled the leftovers from the fridge, and just by looking at the container, the food looked fine. So I cracked open the lid, and as I did, all of the filthy stench of the fires of hell rushed out and flew up my nose.

Now when I smelled that smell, I didn't sit down and start googling "How do I remove the salmon smell from my home?"

I couldn't get the salmon in the trash fast enough.

I took the bag of trash out to the garbage bin, and the garbage truck picked it up shortly after. I opened windows. It still smelled horrible, but I just kept trying things until the smell was gone. It ended up taking several days to rid our house of the salmon stench.

As long as the issues of your heart stay locked in Tupperware, you'll feel no motivation to deal with them.

But as soon as you smell the stink, God has a way of helping you find the next steps to take. We are going to revisit this in the GROW section but let me just get ahead of myself a bit.

YOU CAN'T DO IT ALONE

One of the main truths when it comes to cleaning out the stink that we find in our hearts is that you can't do it alone.

That may look like...

- Bringing that issue to a trusted pastor or friend
- Finding a Christian counselor who can help you with the issue
- Adopting a new spiritual discipline like fasting to help you get perspective

If you're wanting to know the practical steps to take so that Christian community can really help keep you moving in the right direction, know that we'll deep dive into those steps in the GROW chapters.

But for now, just know that seeking help from others is one of the most impactful means of transformation in the Kingdom of God.

When I stepped out of the Atlantic Ocean with Joanna and realized our chairs were nowhere in sight, she was the one who had to calm me down and explain to me that we hadn't been robbed. She was the one who eagle-eyed them and led us back. I had drifted, but she showed me the way back.

Only you can be honest and courageous enough to look inside and see where you've drifted. But usually, only someone else can show you the way back. And that will in large part be the focus of chapters six, seven, and eight. We will learn how to let a loving, compassionate, and wise community help us take what's happening in our hearts and keep us moving toward Jesus.

But before we get there, I want to leave you with this truth.

The reason you keep crashing is because you're leaving your heart on autopilot. And if you really want your life to change, you've got to start digging deeper.

Yes, it might feel scary. And yes, it might be a little painful at first. But I promise the lasting change you'll experience will be worth it.

Let's get digging.

"Throughout my pregnancy, I spent what seemed like every spare moment in prayer, asking God for calm and peace that I knew I wouldn't have within my own mind. And I truly believe that asking God for peace made all the difference."
— Katie Winkler

4

Should I Ask God For Things?

When it comes to how we approach asking God for stuff, I think people fall into one of two camps.

The first camp is for the person who has no problem asking God for every little thing that comes to mind.

They pray for a parking spot when they pull into a crowded lot. They pray that they'll be able to sit next to the really cute person they have a crush on in Spanish class. They pray for the rain to hold off just long enough for their kid's baseball game to end. It doesn't matter how big or how small the request is - this person does not hesitate to ask God for it.

The second camp, I believe, is the more crowded camp.

This camp is for the person who has a hard time asking God for things because they wonder if it's really worth praying about all of the things that are making them feel worried, anxious, or overwhelmed.

Here's the biggest reason why I think the second camp is more crowded.

We have been warned time and again about not seeing God as a vending machine. With a vending machine, you put your dollar in, push a few buttons, and out pops the candy bar you asked for. So many people are tempted to think that God works the same way. If we offer our prayers up, we expect to get what we want.

Because we've heard it said that God isn't here primarily to meet our needs, the pendulum has swung (I believe) way too far in the other direction so that, now, we've become super hesitant to ask God for anything. And we end up not praying about all of the "little things" that "aren't that important."

So by the end of this chapter, I hope we can swing the pendulum back a little closer to the middle.

GOD CARES ABOUT THE SMALLEST SITUATIONS

What I hope to show you or remind you is that God actually wants us to pray about the smallest things. And sometimes the smallest prayers can make the biggest impact.

We see this play out in Scripture when Paul, after being shipwrecked on a strange island, prays a seemingly small prayer that leads to some major life change.

Here's what happens.

There was an estate nearby that belonged to Publius, the chief official of the island. He welcomed us to his home and showed us generous hospitality for three days. His father was sick in bed, suffering from fever and dysentery. Paul went in to see him and, after prayer, placed his hands on him and healed him. When this had happened, the rest of the sick on the island came and were cured. They honored us in many ways; and when we were ready to sail, they furnished us with the supplies we needed (Acts 28:7-10).

Soon after their crash landing, Paul and his companions met the chief official of the island. Paul learns that the chief's father is suffering from a pretty serious illness, so Paul goes to pray for the man.

Now, for some context, Paul had prayed for a lot more serious circumstances in his life than this man's sickness. Paul had encountered a number of near-death experiences that he had prayed through, so to pray for a sickness to be healed probably seemed like a bit of a small prayer to Paul.

However, through Paul's prayers, the chief's father is miraculously healed.

But the story doesn't end there. Once the rest of the islanders hear the news, they bring every sick person they know to Paul so that they, too, can be healed.

As a result, these people experience the love and power of Jesus for the very first time. And not only that, but this tribe ends up providing for Paul and his crew and gives them all of the supplies and provisions they need to survive.

I share this story with you to show you that a small prayer can end up having a huge ripple effect in your life, just like it did in Paul's life.

Or, to put it more simply...

Some of the smallest prayers have the biggest impact.

The same thing is true for you. When you pray for small and seemingly insignificant things, oftentimes there is a ripple effect that goes far beyond what you might imagine.

Let me give you a fairly extreme (and almost laughable) example.

Don't expect this to happen to you every day, but it's just too crazy of a story not to share.

And it is 100% true.

MY CRAZIEST PRAYER STORY

Years back, my little brother was working in retail. He was living on his own, barely making rent, just trying to get by.

My mom's birthday was just around the corner, and he had decided he wanted to buy my mom a pair of shoes that were $99.95. Remember, my brother was barely able to pay his own bills at the time. So needless to say, he didn't have the money to buy the shoes, but he was set on the fact that he was going to get these shoes for our mom.

As he was walking to his car one day, he remembers praying a short, very casual prayer, where he said, "God, I wanna buy these shoes for mom, and I don't know how I'm going to get them. I really don't have 100 bucks to spare. Can you help me out?"

Now, this is the kind of prayer that many people would sort of poke fun at. If there's ever been a "vending machine" prayer, this would be it. "I need money to buy shoes, God. Can you help a brother out?"

Someone might say, "Why pray for shoe money when you should be praying for the starving children around the globe? Or the salvation of the lost? Or the future of the nation? What a selfish and self-centered prayer!"

Nevertheless, this is what my brother prayed for.

So he begins his drive to Nordstrom to purchase the shoes knowing full well that if he buys them, he's not sure how he'll come up with $100 that he'll be short to pay rent.

But as he's driving down the road...

going 30 miles per hour with his windows open...

a $100 bill flew into his car window.

I told you this story was pretty unbelievable.

There was no obvious explanation as to where the bill came from. He wasn't stopped at a red light. No one approached the car. A $100 bill just flew into the window out of nowhere into a rapidly moving vehicle, and it was the exact amount of money my brother needed to buy the shoes for our mom.

My brother prayed a very small prayer, but the Lord answered it, and that experience has had a major impact on my brother's faith to this day. He still says 10 years later that he cannot deny the existence of God after this experience.

Like I said, **some of the smallest prayers have the biggest impact.**

REQUESTS BUILD THE RELATIONSHIP

Now, as I said before, you might have just read that story and thought, "That's an insane example. And it's not going to happen to me." And you may be right about that. But the reality is, when we ask God for things, and He answers in small ways, it will help you build your relationship with God. Because some of the time, He *will* come through in surprising ways.

If you think about it, all relationships require asking the other person for things in order for growth in that relationship to take place.

Think about a couple who is dating.

If the guy looked at the girl one day and said, "Can we just put a regular date on the calendar for all our dates so I don't have to keep asking you out?" that would basically eliminate the romance in the relationship. For that relationship to grow, each member of that dating couple has to continue asking the other person for things.

Imagine that you knew a parent with young kids who organized and trained their kids so well and said, "My goal is that my children never have to ask me for anything." That would destroy the parents' relationship with their little ones because a huge part of a parent-child relationship is dependent on the kids asking the parents for things they need.

To give you one more example, one of the greatest compliments I can ever receive is when people ask me to help them learn to preach. It builds my relationship with that person when they ask me for help.

Our relationship with God is no different. When we ask God for things, our relationship with Him grows and develops. But if we don't ask Him for things, there will be a severely negative impact on our relationship with Him.

After all, God likes to be asked. He wants us to ask Him for help.

God wants you to ask Him to help you as you're wrestling with financial struggles.

God wants you to ask Him for His help when you've lost your job or you want a promotion.

God wants you to ask Him to help you with your struggling marriage.

God wants you to ask Him for His help as you're navigating singleness.

God wants you to ask Him to help you find and live out your purpose.

God wants you to ask Him to help you overcome your battle with sin.

God wants you to ask Him to help you beat an addiction you've been dealing with for years.

No matter how small you might think your request is, God wants you to ask Him about it.

HASN'T GOD ALREADY MADE UP HIS MIND?

Now, you might say, "If God is really all-powerful and all-knowing, isn't He just going to do what He wants anyway? Why should we pray if He already has a plan? Shouldn't we just sit back and wait for God to work it all out the way He sees fit?"

While these are all valid questions, we can see very clearly when we look at Scripture that there is one example after another of people who believe in the power of prayer. And not only did they pray fervently with this belief, but **their prayers did, in fact, make a difference.**

If you want to fact-check me, feel free to go read the following accounts in the Bible:

- Abraham (Genesis 18:16-33)
- Moses (Exodus 32:9-14)
- Hannah (1 Samuel 1:9-20)
- Hezekiah (2 Kings 20:1-11)
- David (Psalm 25:4-5)
- Jonah (Jonah 3:1-10)
- Jesus (Matthew 26:36-46)
- The Early Church (Acts 12:1-17)
- Paul (2 Corinthians 12:7-10)

I'm pretty sure all these people, especially Jesus, knew that God was all-powerful and all-knowing. But they made enough space in their view of God to leave room for mystery. In that place of mystery, they were confident that their prayers could make a difference.

And guess what? They did.

If their prayers mattered, ours do too.

A BALANCED PRAYER BREAKFAST

A lot of us feel like asking God for things is the less healthy part of prayer. We like doing it, but it doesn't feel as mature as praying for the poor and the lost.

We look at asking God for things the same way we look at Cinnamon Toast Crunch.

Do you remember those cereal commercials from years ago that tried to trick us into thinking sugary cereal was good for us? The camera would show a kid chowing down on a bowl of Cinnamon Toast Crunch, and then the next shot would show the bowl of cereal next to a glass of orange juice, some toast, and a plate of scrambled eggs as the voice-over actor said, "Cinnamon Toast Crunch is part of a balanced breakfast."

Deep down, whether we wanted to admit it or not, we knew that statement wasn't true. We knew that the bowl of Cinnamon Toast Crunch had very little to offer us when it came to nutrition. If we were honest with ourselves, the breakfast would be a lot better for us and healthier for us if we removed the sugary cereal from the equation.

Sadly, a lot of us think about asking God for things the same way we view sugary cereal. We think we're holier or we're better Christians if we don't have to ask God for anything.

But friend, that's just a bold-faced lie. Unlike sugary cereals, asking God for things is actually part of a balanced spiritual diet. Our requests to God aren't the cereal, they're the toast, eggs, and orange juice. They're necessary to live healthy spiritual lives. In other words, we can't have a healthy relationship with God without asking Him for the things that are on our hearts.

So, if you're realizing that you fall into camp #2 that we talked about at the beginning of the chapter, I can't stress enough how important it is to bring your requests to God.

Your prayers matter. They make a difference - in your life, in the lives of the people around you, and in your relationship with God.

No matter how big or small the request, it's worth it to talk to Jesus about it.

The fastest way to change your life requires learning to ask God for small things.

As you ask for the small things, you'll start to see Him show up in big ways.

Your faith will start to grow, and your life will start to change.

"Spending time with God brought me peace at a time when my life felt like it was falling apart. It has helped me discover humility and made me better able to love other people. I don't worry so much. I feel safe. I feel purpose. I can better sense what He wants for me and why I'm here." — Keegan Frank

5

One Trip To The Roof

When I was a kid, my parents were always telling me to do my "quiet time." You might have heard this term before. Basically, this was a time set aside to be quiet and be alone with God. I believed that at least part of that process was supposed to include waiting to see if God would speak directly to you.

But I also thought, "That's never really gonna happen."

I remember thinking, "What's the difference between a 'quiet time' and a 'time-out?'"

You're telling me that if I get in trouble, I have to sit alone and be quiet?

AND

...if I want to have a relationship with Jesus, I also need to sit alone and be quiet?

Sounds like growing spiritually is more of a punishment than a privilege.

I think most adults feel the same way. The idea of sitting in stillness listening for God's voice feels like a toll you have to pay to stay on the highway of Christianity.

Maybe you tried having a quiet time for a while, and you felt nothing.

You got up and went back to your messy life filled with issues...issues in your marriage, your dating life, your singleness, your parenting, your job, your anxiety and depression, and the list keeps going.

But maybe you tried again the next day.

Sat.

Listened.

Still nothing.

You tried day three, and day four. And maybe even day five.

But after all that time of nothing changing, you gave up and said maybe that part of spending time with Jesus is the optional part.

Now, I don't want to promise you that there's a secret formula to hear the voice of God on a daily basis. Just like lifting weights or learning piano or discovering how to cook, it takes a little bit of effort every day to make progress.

In the same way, the primary value of spending time in stillness with God is in the little incremental changes it brings inside us.

But in this chapter, I want to talk about the reality that there **WILL** be breakthrough days.

The fireworks will go off. There will be "aha" moments. There will be days when your whole world turns on its axis because you chose to spend time with God that day, and on that day, He chose to speak.

But in order for this to happen, you have to spend time with God consistently.

Daily discipline leads to life-changing breakthrough moments.

When you're consistent with your quiet time, I can assure you that you will have times of world-changing messages from the voice of God, like the one Peter had in Acts 10.

THE BACKGROUND TO THE BREAKTHROUGH

Before we dive into Peter's breakthrough moment, let me give you some background.

Even though Jesus made it clear He died for the sins of the whole world, most early Christians were of Jewish heritage. Due to a bunch of complicated social factors, the entire early Christian church believed wholeheartedly that the good news about Jesus was *only* meant for Jewish people.

If that way of thinking hadn't changed over the course of history, Christianity would have stayed an only-for-the-Jews religion and (assuming that you aren't Jewish) you would not know that Jesus loved you, died for you, and wants a relationship with you.

How did that Jewish-centric mindset change? How did Christianity end up spreading across the entire planet? Why did you have a chance to meet Jesus?

Because of Peter's time with God on a single day 2,000 years ago.

Here's what happened.

PETER'S BREAKTHROUGH DAY

As a reminder, Peter was one of Jesus' 12 disciples, His closest community. Peter was also the man on whom Jesus said He would build His church (Matthew 16:18). So Peter was a very well-known figure in the early church. But he was also in the very same state of mind as the rest of the church. He thought Jesus was only for the Jews.

With all of that in mind, let's look at an account of one of Peter's quiet times described in Acts 10.

About noon the following day as they were on their journey and approaching the city, Peter went up on the roof to pray. He became hungry and wanted something to eat, and while the meal was being prepared, he fell into a trance (Acts 10:9-10).

I love that the story includes the fact that Peter was hungry. He got distracted just like we do. Mid-prayer session, he starts to think "I should've had breakfast first." Maybe he even thought about skipping his quiet time for the day, but for whatever reason, he decided to push through and continue with his time in prayer. And as he does, on this particular day, God decides to speak. And Peter falls into a trance (a vision from God).

Let's keep reading.

He saw heaven opened and something like a large sheet being let down to earth by its four corners. It contained all kinds of four-footed animals, as well as reptiles and birds. Then a voice told him, "Get up, Peter. Kill and eat." "Surely not, Lord!" Peter replied. "I have never eaten anything impure or unclean." The voice spoke to him a second time, "Do not call anything impure that God has made clean" (Acts 10:11-15).

Now, I get this might seem a little confusing. Why in the world would God give Peter a vision of animals on a big sheet? But as the story continues, Peter realizes that God wasn't talking about animals. He was talking about the Gentiles (non-Jewish people).

The Jews were so quick to consider the Gentiles unclean and that's why they weren't sharing the gospel with them. But when Jesus died, He died for *everyone*. He gave *everyone* the chance to be cleansed from their sins, including the Gentiles.

Next thing you know, a non-Jewish dude shows up at the door and asks Peter if he's willing to come talk to a bunch of non-Jewish people about Jesus.

If Peter hadn't taken time to listen to the voice of God that day, he would certainly have said no. Jews weren't even supposed to eat with Gentiles.

But because of the vision, he says yes. He talks to them about Jesus. God shows up in a powerful way and a bunch of Gentiles get saved. Peter's mind is blown. He brings the news back to the leaders of the church and they all realize how wrong they were being to keep Jesus to themselves.

Suddenly, their eyes are opened, and they remember all the stuff Jesus said about loving EVERYONE. And the gospel begins to spread beyond the boundaries of the Jewish culture.

A QUIET TIME CHAIN REACTION

Don't miss the chain of events.

If Peter hadn't sat quietly with God on top of the roof that day, the gospel would have remained trapped in one people group, and there's a high probability that you wouldn't even know who Jesus was or what He did for you on the cross.

The world was changed forever because Peter was faithful and obedient to have his quiet time that day.

Think about it this way.

God can change the whole world through one trip to the roof.

God can change the whole world through one time listening for His voice.

God can change the whole world through one person's quiet time.

Let me promise you two things.

Firstly, I promise you that this sort of life-changing moment is not going to happen to you every time you sit down to pray and read the Bible.

Secondly, I promise you that *sometimes* it will.

I've had a handful of these moments over the years. Moments where the presence of God showed up so powerfully my entire body shook uncontrollably for 10 minutes. Moments where God convicted me so deeply of sin that I took action and never looked back. Moments where God spoke so clearly I knew I had to make major life-changing decisions. Let me tell you about one of those moments.

A DIRECTION-CHANGING TRIP TO THE ROOF

Before I became a Christian, I had played in semi-professional bands for a long time. I had written songs and felt gifted to play music. When I became a Christian, I assumed that God would want me to take that musical gift and use it to serve Him. The natural step seemed obvious that I should become a worship leader.

I had played guitar but had never been a singer, and to be honest, I stunk at it. I was not cover-your-ears-bad, but I was definitely hey-can-you-skip-to-the-next-song bad.

But I was utterly determined and embarked on a multi-year journey of learning how to sing.

I spent thousands of dollars on voice lessons and hundreds of hours practicing, but I never really made much progress.

I was very, very frustrated and confused.

One particular day, I sat down to do my quiet time and just started yelling at God. "God, I gave up a LOT to follow you. You gifted me for music. All I want to do is serve you by leading your people in worship. Why isn't this working?"

At that exact moment, it was as if someone had switched on an overhead projector in my head, and the words "1 Chronicles 15" appeared in my brain.

I had never really experienced that before and was a little freaked out.

I was also confused because I had no recollection whatsoever of what 1 Chronicles 15 was about. Some random Old Testament passage right? But I pulled out my Bible and started reading and here's what I found in 1 Chronicles 15:22.

"Kenaniah the head Levite was in charge of the singing; that was his responsibility because he was skillful at it."

Don't miss this.

1 Chronicles 15:22 is probably the *only* verse in the Bible that talks about someone who had the job of singing for God, and it specifically says that it was his job because he was a good singer.

I had never heard this verse before, and my jaw dropped.

This may not sound like the biggest miracle to you, but it was one of the biggest for me. God put a Scripture reference in my head that spoke to my situation in a specific way, and it was utterly miraculous because I had never read it before.

And in that moment, I also heard God whisper, "It's okay to let that dream die."

It took some time to fully accept that God had called me to preach and not to sing, but that moment was the defining moment of the entire direction and purpose of my life.

And it all happened because I decided one day to sit down and listen for the voice of God - to do my quiet time.

Those sorts of miraculous, life-changing moments will happen for you too.

But they will happen when you make spending time with God a discipline.

DAILY DISCIPLINE LEADS TO BREAKTHROUGH

Listen, God is not a magic eight ball, a fortune teller, or a tarot card reader. He doesn't perform on command. He expects us to lean in again and again and again. To embrace discipline. And He rewards our efforts when He sees fit, not when we do.

If you want to see a shooting star, you can't glance up at the sky for five minutes every few weeks and expect to see one. You have to make sitting and looking up a *discipline*.

Or, you know those weird bird watcher people? No offense if that's you. They don't glance out their window every now and then and expect to see something beautiful and rare.

Or if you're a surfer, you don't quit surfing because the perfect conditions don't come every day. You take what you have each morning and look forward to the occasional best waves.

Spending time with God works the same way. You have to do it consistently to have the shooting star moments, the beautiful bird moments, the perfect wave moments.

Maybe this seems unfair.

Why didn't God give me my shooting star 1 Chronicles 15 moment earlier?

I don't know.

But Peter's vision didn't come to him the first time he had a quiet time either.

And I do believe with all my heart that my moment, and all those other moments, wouldn't have happened if I hadn't been sitting down and looking up at the sky and waiting for something beautiful on a regular basis.

So where do we go from here?

Well, let's answer that question with a question.

WHERE'S YOUR ROOF?

Do you have a roof?

Do you have a place where you go to be still and listen to the voice of God?

Do you have a chair you sit in? A basement closet? A commute to work?

Do you have a roof?

That's your first step. That's what you've got to figure out before anything else. You've got to have a roof.

The fastest way to change your life requires learning to regularly go to the roof.

Because if you go there regularly...

God can change your marriage through one trip to the roof.

God can change your relationship with your kids through one trip to the roof.

God can change your purpose, bring back your fire, show you a new direction if you will just get in His presence and take a trip to the roof.

Like we said before, there's value in the small steps of obedience...the little changes that God brings into our hearts through consistent time in his presence.

BUT ALSO!

Don't miss your moment.

Don't miss your chance to connect with God each and every day.

God's direction and guidance for you is meant to happen daily.

And today just might be your day.

For more tips on how to have a daily quiet time, check out our Quiet Time Guide on page 167.

GROW

"Having Christian friends has helped me grow in so many ways! They love me, encourage me, and hold me accountable when I need it. There's something really powerful about honestly sharing with my friends what is going on in my life spiritually, emotionally, and physically." - *Emily Cropper*

6

Fast Food Friendships

For a lot of you, these next few chapters may be the toughest part of the book.

The constant slogan of modern Christianity is "You need a personal relationship with Jesus." What does that mean in a nutshell? Go to church, read your Bible, and pray.

I agree with that slogan 100%.

And as you saw in the last few chapters, I desperately want you to go to church, read your Bible, and pray.

But here's what I also believe 100%.

If your faith begins and ends with your personal relationship with Jesus, you will stay stuck, and your life won't change.

To put it another way, knowing God is enough to get you to heaven.

But it's not enough for spiritual growth.

In order to grow, you also need good people around you.

You might think I'm saying that because my faith in the power of God to change your life is weak. But that isn't why.

I'm saying you need good people around you because that is also what God says. As you'll see later in the chapter, even the strongest Christians need good people around them.

If you want to change your life, and if you want that change to happen as quickly as possible, God is saying to you right now "You need a relationship with me. But you also need a team of people to help you walk the path of life."

You need to **KNOW** God, but you also need to **GROW** in a community of other Christians.

For the next three chapters, we're going to talk about the why and the how of building a community of people around you to help you walk with Jesus.

FAST FOOD FRIENDSHIPS

Let's begin with addressing one of the biggest problems when it comes to friendships so that you can move toward the life change you're looking for.

This is a problem I like to refer to as **fast food friendships.**

If you'll remember from back in Chapter 2, I love a good double cheeseburger from McDonald's. They are one of my favorite things to eat on the whole planet. And I prefer to eat them with Big Mac sauce. I can feel your judgment flowing back in time toward me even as I write this sentence but don't knock it 'til you try it.

I could eat a McDonald's double cheeseburger for breakfast, lunch, and dinner every day of the week. They are just that good.

Now stay with me.

Yes, McDonald's is not healthy food, but for some bizarre reason, if it was the only food left on planet Earth, McDonald's would be better than starvation. McDonald's will keep you alive.

But if I were to eat those double cheeseburgers for every single meal for the rest of my life, that could *also* kill me. It's not healthy in the long run for me to only consume fast food.

The same is true when it comes to our friendships.

Having no friends will kill you spiritually.

There have been countless studies on the damaging effects on kids (or adults) who live their lives in isolation. There's no doubt about that.

But having certain friendships will also kill you spiritually.

These friendships are what I like to call fast food friendships. Yes, it is better to have fast food friends than no friends, but fast food friends will also destroy your path of personal growth and change.

THE RECIPE FOR FAST FOOD FRIENDS

So what defines a fast food friend?

Here are the two main ingredients.

1. Vagueness

The first characteristic of a fast food friendship is **vagueness**. It's a relationship where everything stays surface-level. No one gets deep. No one opens up. No one chooses to be vulnerable.

This could look like you asking your friend how they're doing, and they respond with, "Well, I could really use some prayer. My marriage is kind of struggling."

At this point, you might ask a follow-up question, trying to get some more context, but all your friend can seem to do is give you vague answers and unclear statements without ever really opening up about what's going on in their life. They say things like:

"I've just been feeling a little anxious lately."

"I feel like I'm in a funk, but I'll get over it."

"Parenting is tough, but I know it's just a season."

"Life is just hard, you know?"

These types of statements are very common in fast food friendships.

If the friendship ever does become more transparent, you will find yourself with ingredient number two.

2. Unconditional approval

At first glance, unconditional approval might sound like a great friendship quality. After all, who wouldn't want unconditional approval? But while it might seem like a good thing on the surface, if you're trying to change your life, having a bunch of "yes-men" around you at all times is a recipe for disaster.

Fast food friends are the type of friends that never push back. They don't hold you accountable or ask you the hard questions. Instead, they live according to the mantra, "Do whatever makes you happy."

Here's what unconditional approval sounds like...

I'm gonna quit therapy. // You never really liked that therapist anyway!

I'm getting back together with my ex. // You need to do what makes you happy.

I'm quitting my job. // I'm sure there's a better one just around the corner!

I'm thinking about robbing a bank. // You do you, boo boo!

Okay, the last one is probably an exaggeration. But do you see the picture I'm trying to paint? Fast food friends tell you whatever you want to hear.

It feels good in the moment, but it will kill you in the long run.

Here's the bad news...many fast food friends don't really care about you. They just care about making you feel good and avoiding conflict at all costs.

It might feel good to have fast food friends in certain moments. But if all you have are fast food friends, over time, just like those McDonald's double cheeseburgers, they'll kill you spiritually.

The only reason for having friendships that only affirm you is if you're perfect, if you're just like Jesus, and if all your friends are perfect and exactly like Jesus.

And if that's you, then you should probably just go ahead and put this book down because you don't need it.

For the rest of us - the flawed, imperfect human beings - we need more than fast food friendships.

AIN'T NOBODY GOING TO TELL ME WHAT TO DO

Now you might say, "I don't need anyone telling me what to do. I want to change my life and follow Jesus, but I can figure it out on my own. I don't need anyone holding me accountable or correcting my choices."

If that's you, I want to tell you about Peter. If there was anyone who you think wouldn't need correction or accountability from other people, it would be Peter.

First of all, Peter had already been corrected several times by Jesus Himself. For instance, Peter denied that he knew Jesus three different times during the crucifixion, and he was later called out for that by Jesus. At one point, Jesus even looked Peter in the face and said, "Get behind me, Satan." If that's not challenging someone, I don't know what is. So Peter had experienced his fair share of accountability directly from Jesus.

On top of that, Peter was one of Jesus' closest friends. Not only was Peter one of the original 12 disciples, but he was in the top tier of the friend group, Jesus' inner circle of three made up of Peter, James, and John. So he had a closer friendship with Jesus than most people ever will.

Additionally, Peter was a key leader (if not *the* key leader) of the church of Jerusalem. He preached sermons where he led thousands of people to Christ. He had a major impact on the initial growth of Christianity.

One of the coolest parts of Peter's story is that he was the main player in uniting the early church across all ethnic lines.

As someone who grew up Jewish, Peter had been taught that it was wrong to have any interaction with non-Jewish people. But as we read in the last chapter, after Peter put his faith in Jesus, God gave Peter a special vision showing that there was meant to be no division between Jews and Gentiles. Peter shared this vision with the earlier church leaders, paving the way for the rest of the church to follow his example.

Cool right?

HOW PETER BLEW IT

Well...even though Peter was a leader of change, apparently, he fell back into his old ways.

Check out this little excerpt from a letter written by another key leader in the church, the Apostle Paul. Paul writes about a run-in he had with Peter *after* Peter had already become a champion for racial inclusion in the church.

"When Cephas [another name for Peter] came to Antioch, I opposed him to his face, because he stood condemned. For before certain men came from James, he used to eat with the Gentiles. But when they arrived, he began to draw back and separate himself from the Gentiles because he was afraid of those who belonged to the circumcision group. The other Jews joined him in his hypocrisy, so that by their hypocrisy even Barnabas was led astray (Galatians 2:11-13).

What's going on here?

Despite the fact that Peter had been a champion for the Gentiles to be included in the church, when certain groups of people started peer-pressuring Peter to go back to Jewish customs and quit hanging out with Gentiles, Peter went back on everything he had said. He pulled away from his Gentile friendships and started focusing only on relationships with other Jews. And then according to Paul, the same way people followed Peter toward racial inclusion, they also followed Peter back into division.

Peter started strong, but he needed correction from Paul.

Now don't miss this. This confrontation between Paul and Peter didn't happen early on in Peter's journey. It happened after Peter was already a very, very mature and grounded leader in the church.

Despite all his progress and his deep connection to Jesus, Peter still needed someone to call him out.

Here's the point.

There is no level of maturity that no longer requires accountability.

If Peter needed correction, not just from God, but from other humans, then so do all of us.

If Peter can get off track, you can get off track in your marriage, your finances, your parenting, your recovery, your relationship with Jesus, and so many other things.

When we get off track, sometimes God will redirect us Himself. But sometimes, God will use other people to get us on the right path.

Peter had Paul to call him out and hold him accountable. And you're going to need friends like Paul, too.

FITNESS FRIENDSHIPS

You need **fitness friends**.

Fitness friends are the exact opposite of fast food friends.

Fitness friends are defined by two things as well, and they're the opposite of what defines fast food friends.

Fast food friends keep things **vague**. Fitness friends keep things **vulnerable**.

Fast food friends practice unconditional **approval**. Fitness friends practice **accountability**.

If you're looking for the fastest way to change your life, you're going to need fitness friendships.

Let me try to give you a picture of what a fitness friendship looks like.

SCARY BUT NECESSARY

In 2011, I wrestled with a fairly serious eating disorder. I was in a very broken place mentally. There were a lot of issues from my childhood that I had yet to deal with. And through a series of triggering life circumstances, I fell into something I never would have imagined.

At the peak of my struggle with this disorder, I was running an hour a day, eating 1200 calories, and weighed about 50 pounds less than what I would consider my ideal weight.

I was skin and bones and still thought I weighed too much.

When enough friends started confronting me about what was going on (we could write a whole chapter on these fitness friends) I began to open myself up to the possibility that something wasn't right. And I eventually started going to counseling and seeing a therapist.

After several months of counseling, I started eating again and realized I needed to rebuild my body.

At that time, I was living with a guy who was very much into fitness and working out.

The guy was practically made of muscle. He was a foot taller than me and looked like a bodybuilder. He also owned a restaurant and was used to telling people what to do.

Which is what he started doing with me.

While we were living together and I was at the beginning of my health journey, my roommate took it upon himself (without me asking, mind you) to help me rebuild my body and get back to a healthy weight.

We went to the gym together every single day, solely lifting weights so that I could start putting on muscle and gaining back the weight I needed to get to a healthier place.

The entire time we were doing this, my roommate was IN MY BUSINESS.

He would wake me up every morning practically screaming, "You ready to go to the gym, Vince? Let's go!!!" There were so many mornings where I groaned with absolutely zero motivation to go to the gym. But he was relentless.

Once we got to the gym each day, he didn't just leave me to figure things out on my own while he went and did his own thing for a couple of hours.

No, he basically held my hand the entire way, telling me which exercises to do, spotting me, helping me figure out how much weight I needed to be lifting and how many reps I needed to do.

He was right there with me the entire time, constantly checking in on me and holding me accountable. And that made all the difference.

Yes, I was in therapy at the time as well, and it was super helpful during that season of my life.

But I am convinced that I wouldn't have stayed on the path the way I did if I didn't have someone like my roommate kicking my butt and holding me accountable every step of the way.

To be honest, there were a lot of days I didn't really like my roommate. I was maybe even afraid of him at times. But I don't think I would have gotten back to a healthy weight if it hadn't been for him.

Here's how you know whether or not you've got any fitness friendships.

They're going to feel a little scary, but also very necessary.

It's scary to have people in your business.

People who...

- push you
- check in on you
- hold you accountable
- ask you the hard questions

But it is also necessary to have people who know what's really going on in your life, down to the details.

How many friends do you have like this?

If your life needs to change, my guess would be that you have zero.

The fastest way to change your life includes finding some fitness friendships.

Because when you let fitness friends have access to your life, it's hard to stay stuck for long.

But how do we find friends like this?

Well, that leads us to our next big idea.

CONFESSION IS THE KEY

Now, I know what you're thinking.

"But Vince, I already confess to God! Why do I have to confess to other people too?"

That's a very common response I get when I talk to people about confessing in community. But Scripture actually addresses this very clearly. James 5:16 says, *"Therefore confess your sins to each other and pray for each other so that you may be healed. The prayer of a righteous person is powerful and effective."*

Just to be clear, when it comes to confessing sins, the only person you have to confess your sins to in order to receive forgiveness is Jesus. Confessing your sins to other people is **not** required for forgiveness.

But if you want to experience healing, if you want your life to change, if you want to overcome your struggles, God is telling us through His Word that we're going to have to confess to other people. There is no other way around it.

No one is going to be able to challenge you or hold you accountable if they don't even know what's going on behind closed doors.

Here are two big, simple, and incredibly difficult steps you need to take if you want to have fitness friendships.

THE LAST 2%

When we start to open up with others within community, it can be tempting to be selective in what we share. We share a little bit at first, then we share a little bit more, but internally we decide that there's one little piece we're going to keep to ourselves. It's just easier that way.

Here's the reality: **the more you can be real, the more you will heal.** That means sharing the last 2% that you're tempted to keep to yourself.

During my time as a pastor, I've heard a lot of guys say, "I'm struggling with purity." That's what I would consider as sharing the first 50%.

Then eventually, they'll open up some more and say, "I'm struggling with pornography." That would be getting to 98%.

The last 2% would be sharing how often they're looking at pornography. It's a tough detail to share, but that's where the accountability can truly begin.

The same thing can be true with drinking. First, someone might share that they're struggling with self-control. That's 50%.

Then they open up and say they've been drinking too much. That's 48%.

The last 2% would be sharing that they're getting drunk every weekend or that they're drinking five beers every night.

It's easy to share the first 50%. And sometimes it's even easy to share the next 48%. The toughest part to share often lies in that last 2%.

But that 2% is where *all* the freedom starts.

PROACTIVE ACCOUNTABILITY

If you've got a friend like my roommate who will take the initiative to keep you moving in the right direction, that's great. But friends who are that bold are extremely hard to find.

If you want a fitness friend, you're going to have to ask them to be that fitness friend to you. Meaning, you have to commit to proactively keep telling that person what you're struggling with and actively asking them to hold you accountable.

Let's say you've been dealing with some back pain. So you go to the doctor and as he's examining you, he notices some things that are wrong. He might notice you've got a Band-Aid on your finger, or there's a bruise on your knee, or your throat is red and swollen.

But if the doctor doesn't notice that something is wrong with your back, you wouldn't just leave your appointment without telling him you've been dealing with back pain, right?

No! You would proactively communicate to your doctor that your back has been hurting. You share with him the things that he might not be able to see on the surface so he can help you heal.

The same is true for confessing in community. We have to proactively let others know what's going on in our lives - how we're hurting, how we're struggling - especially when it's things that wouldn't necessarily be seen on the surface.

The more you open up, the more you choose to be vulnerable, and the more you let others in, the more healing, freedom, victory, and life change you're going to experience.

WHO ARE YOU SURROUNDED BY?

I don't want you to live a life filled with fast food friendships. I want you to be surrounded by fitness friends. I want you to experience the freedom and victory that come as a result of being held accountable by those closest to you.

I know it's scary. But it's also necessary if you want God to change your life.

Remember, there is no level of maturity that no longer requires accountability.

You need good friends. You need the right friends. You need fitness friends.

When I first joined my small group, I came in a mess of postpartum depression and anxiety. I was so afraid to tell people what was truly happening in my life for fear of judgment and abandonment. But when I finally opened up and told my group my deepest sorrows and greatest joys, they loved me through it all. It's been such a blessing to experience the love of Christ through other people. I can't imagine living life now without the support of my small group. – Courtney Mitchell

7

How To Make Friends

As I'm currently writing this book, my wife is weeks away from giving birth to our first child, Lucy. You can imagine all of the things that are running through my head as I prepare to become a dad and raise our little girl. One thing I've specifically been thinking about is all of the things I want to help little Lucy learn as she grows up.

I want to teach her how to count to ten, how to say "Dada," how to give people high-fives so she's prepared when I ask our congregation to give high-fives to people around them every Sunday morning before I start preaching.

You know, the simple stuff.

I'm also really excited to teach Lucy how to ride a bike. I remember how fun it was when my parents taught me how to ride a bicycle when I was growing up, and I am excited to create that memory for my daughter too.

Now, I want you to imagine if three weeks after Lucy was born, I decided I was going to start teaching my daughter how to ride a bike.

Start 'em young, am I right?

Why would that be a terrible idea?

Because there are steps in place for a baby to learn to take so that when it comes time for her to ride a bike, she's better prepared. First babies wiggle. Then they roll over. Then comes crawling, standing up, waddling. Then before you know it, they're walking. From there, they can start learning how to ride a tricycle. Then training wheels. And when they think they've finally mastered that, they can graduate to learning to ride a bike without the training wheels.

There are a lot of steps between a baby lying immobile and a child riding a bike.

Building relationships and friendships is one of the most important skills we need to learn as human beings.

And yet, for most people, when it comes to friendships, we are required to go from lying immobile to riding a bicycle with absolutely no steps in between.

Think about it. For the first 18 years of our lives, we are spoon-fed friendships. When you're a toddler, you have siblings, daycare buddies, or your parents' friends' kids to play with. Then you start kindergarten, and from that point until you graduate high school, there are countless relationship onramps. These onramps include sports, clubs, church, youth group, dances, committees, video games, and social media. You are naturally put in close proximity with people in your exact age, stage, and situation.

It's nearly impossible to NOT make friends.

But once you graduate high school, or even college (if you decide to go), and you finally join the workforce, all of a sudden, all the onramps are gone.

Friendships are no longer handed to us, and we're not sure what to do about it.

The beginning of joining the workforce is, for most people, the end of finding friends.

What do I do...walk up to the dude in the cubicle next to me and ask him to be my friend?

For a long time, people just stayed friends with people from high school, but in our increasingly transient culture, that's becoming more and more rare.

There are no friendship training wheels, and this is the first problem when it comes to finding friends.

THE FRIENDSHIP BYSTANDER EFFECT

The second problem is that everyone thinks someone else is going to fix the first problem.

This is what's called the bystander effect. You may have never heard of it, but it is a very real thing.

There have been countless true stories in which someone is walking down a street when, all of a sudden, they are mugged in broad daylight. The weird thing is that everyone around this person is watching the mugging take place - from the windows, from across the street - and no one does anything to help.

Why? Because they're all heartless? No, because they assume someone else is going to step in.

They're thinking, "Surely someone else is already calling 911. Surely someone else is going to help that person. Surely someone else is going to step in." But nothing happens because everyone is operating as a bystander.

I think the bystander effect is in full swing when it comes to friendships, ESPECIALLY at church.

We come in, take a seat amongst the other hundreds of people in the room, and look around thinking "I hope I become friends with these people."

But years go by, and everyone stays strangers. Nothing happens because everyone thinks someone else is going to initiate the friendship-building process.

The hard reality we need to come to grips with is that no one is going to fix this for us.

COMMUNITY CREATORS

No one is going to spoon-feed us friendships the way they did when we were kids. If we want friends, we're going to have to do something about it.

But I think this is something we can learn to do.

It's a big jump from baby mode to riding a bike, but I believe we can make the leap.

Just like Lydia did in the Book of Acts.

Lydia was one of the many people to step into a relationship with Jesus after hearing Paul preach the gospel. Acts 16 tells the story of the day that Lydia accepted Christ, *"On the Sabbath we went outside the city gate to the river, where we expected to find a place of prayer. We sat down and began to speak to the women who had gathered there. One of those listening was a woman from the city of Thyatira named Lydia, a dealer in purple cloth. She was a worshiper of God. The Lord opened her heart to respond to Paul's message"* (Acts 16:13-14).

But the story of Lydia doesn't stop with her salvation. Immediately, once Lydia accepts Jesus, she springs into action to make friends and find community.

When she and the members of her household were baptized, she invited us to her home. "If you consider me a believer in the Lord," she said, "come and stay at my house." And she persuaded us (Acts 16:15).

Lydia didn't take a passive approach to relationships.

She did not fall prey to the bystander effect.

Instead, she practically *demanded* to be friends with Paul and Timothy.

"Hi guys. I don't know you. You don't really know me. But you're coming over today."

Lydia essentially said, "You will now become my friends."

Can you imagine how scary it would be to walk up to the apostles who just led you to Jesus and demand that they come stay at your house and become your friends? How terrifying and intimidating would that feel?

But Lydia wasn't letting anything stop her. She took radical initiative in order to create friendships.

And she didn't stop with Paul and Timothy. As you read in Acts 16, you'll see that Lydia not only invited Paul and Timothy to her house multiple times, but she eventually started hosting an entire gathering of believers at her house on a regular basis (Acts 16:40).

The point I'm trying to make clear to you with this story is that Lydia didn't look for people to befriend her.

She became a friend to people.

Lydia didn't look for community.

She created community.

And if you and I are going to find meaningful, godly friendships, we're going to have to learn to follow Lydia's example.

WHY EVERYONE IS FRIENDSHIP DRAINED

How do we do this on a practical level?

At our church, the Bridge, we are constantly preaching to people about the importance of friendships and community. The main way we connect with each other is by joining a small group.

That's the main action step I hope you take after reading this chapter. But I also want you to know that joining a small group is not the miracle cure. It all depends on how you show up when you join a small group. One of the most tragic things is when a group of people commit to a small group, and they STILL don't become friends.

Here's why I think that happens.

The new MacBooks have a charging port for what's called a USB-C cable. This cable, on one end, plugs into the MacBook, and the other end plugs into the charging brick that goes into the wall. Both ends of the cable are identical. The end that plugs into the charging brick is exactly the same as the end that plugs into the computer.

So in theory, you could put eight MacBooks in a circle, connect them to each other with these USB-C cables, and say, "Look, we've plugged all of these MacBooks into each other! How cool is that? Now they're all going to be charging each other up! I'll never have to pay an electric bill again!"

But the reality is, if you connect all of these MacBooks to each other, they're not going to stay charged because they're actually draining power from each other.

That so often happens in small groups.

You sit in a circle in a small group, and you're connected to each other, but everyone leaves feeling drained rather than feeling energized.

Why?

Because everyone is expecting everyone else to charge them up.

Everybody is hoping for someone...

- to talk to them
- to befriend them
- to get to know them
- to show an interest in them
- to ask them questions

but it just doesn't happen.

Why? Because everyone is waiting for everyone else to make the first move. It's just the bystander effect AGAIN but on a micro-scale.

Everyone is waiting to find a friend, but no one knows how to be a friend.

Just like if you plugged a bunch of MacBooks into each other expecting them to charge each other, when in fact they ended up draining each other.

If you're trying to find the fastest way to change your life, you'll need to find an effective way to build healthy friendships.

FRIENDSHIP POWER TOOLS

In the remaining paragraphs, I cannot give you a full explanation of how to make friends.

But I do want to give you one practical tool to get you started. If you start using this tool, a lot of the other friendship pieces will fall into place.

You're probably going to think this tool is too simple, but trust me, it is a power tool. And it will get you a lot further than you think.

The friendship power tool is this: You must learn to engage in asking questions and become an active listener.

That's it.

Ask questions and listen well.

David Augsburger, the author of *Caring Enough To Hear and Be Heard*, said something that haunts me about listening. He said, "Being heard is so close to being loved that for the average person, they are almost indistinguishable."

When someone sits down and truly listens to you and takes an interest in your life, you will walk away thinking, "What a great person. I hope we can talk again."

Guess what?

You may never find someone who does that for you.

But you can do it for others.

Active listening is often the first practical manifestation of love that someone feels in a relationship. Active listening is often the sustaining manifestation of love that keeps a relationship strong.

So, for the rest of this chapter, we're not going to talk about how you can find a friend, but how you can become a friend - not by waiting for someone to talk to you, but instead by learning how to talk to other people.

WHAT FRIENDSHIP SOUNDS LIKE

I believe that building strong friendships is a lot like playing catch. Playing catch doesn't work if one person throws the ball but then the other person lets the ball drop every time. A good game of catch is enjoyed when both people are throwing the ball *and* catching it.

In friendship, this means when you ask a question, it's important to let the other person know you caught the answer.

Here's what that sounds like.

You could ask, "What's something you're struggling with at work right now?" They might say something like, "Well, my boss is really coming down on me about not meeting deadlines."

When you hear their response, all you have to do is say something that demonstrates you caught the answer. That response can be basically anything (except just turning the conversation and talking about yourself.)

Maybe you say...

"Wow, that sounds like it must be tough for you."

"Wow, it sounds like your boss is being pretty hard on you."

"Wow, so what do you think your next steps are in light of that pressure you're dealing with?"

Anything that says, "You threw the ball my way and I caught it."

Whatever it is - asking a follow-up question, repeating what you heard, rephrasing their response - you have to let them know that you caught what they said.

You might have to coach the other person a bit so they will begin to do the same for you. But it will happen. They will start to mirror your behavior. And before you know it, you're having deep, meaningful, vulnerable conversations, and you're building lasting friendships.

YES, IT'S REALLY THAT SIMPLE

There are other friendship skills we could talk about beyond the scope of this book.

But believe it or not, if all you learn to do is ask questions and tell people you caught the answer, you will make friends, guaranteed.

- People will rave about what a great and compassionate listener and friend you are.
- You may find yourself promoted at work.
- You might get put into leadership positions at church.
- You may even end up on the news.

Okay, the news thing is a joke, but all the other stuff has turned out to be 100% true for many, many people.

So ask questions.

Let people know you caught the answers.

If you take these practical steps, you'll no longer find yourself waiting for community to find you. You'll start creating community for yourself.

"Being open with the other guys in my small group isn't always comfortable, but it always leads to me feeling closer to the group and closer to God." – Brian Davis

8

Don't Get Struck Dead

Even if you 100% bought into the last two chapters you just read, if you're like most people, it's easy to let building Christian friendships drop to the bottom of your to-do list.

We want friends, but now's just too busy of a season.

Often, making Christian friends feels as important to us as swapping out the tires on my car feels to me.

I've never understood when you *really* need to get new tires on a car. Actually, I've never really understood much of anything about cars, but the tire thing especially gets me.

I'll stop in for an oil change and the guy will say, "Getting pretty bald." And at first, I'll think, "I know man, my 40s are right around the corner."

But then I realize he's talking about the tires, not my hairline.

The *treads* are bald. I'll often think, "Okay man, you're the expert, put them on." But then I pause and wonder, "What would really happen if I waited another six months? How about a year? How about two?

Would I crash?

Would they all pop?

Would I slide right off the road?

Will the tire police arrest me?

I know, I know. I'll need them eventually.

But can't I just wait a little longer?"

And usually...I do.

That's often how we think about finding good Christian friends.

I know I need them eventually. But can't I wait just a little longer? Will the friendship police arrest me if I wait?

I'll wait until this work project slows down, or the kids finish soccer, or this season of The Bachelor ends, or until I actually go bald.

But I'll be fine on my own for a little longer.

DOES GOD CARE WHETHER OR NOT I HAVE FRIENDS?

Most of us assume that as long as we're not being directly disobedient to God in our personal lives, He doesn't really care much about what our relationships with other believers look like.

Most of us assume that God is sort of like a high school teacher. As long as you're getting good grades, it's fine to sit at the back of the class and keep to yourself.

In my last year of high school, I had an elective with a teacher that everyone loved who we'll call Mrs. T.

The class with Mrs. T was basically a blow-off class, and I was the only senior. The rest of the class were freshmen and sophomores. Despite liking Mrs. T, it was also the first period of the day, and I would often doze in the back.

I didn't really make an effort to talk to any of the other students, even though a lot of them wanted to be friends with the only senior in the room.

I was never outrightly mean to them; I knew Mrs. T wouldn't have been okay with open mistreatment. But I just really didn't care about getting to know any of them.

On the last day of senior year, the class and Mrs. T orchestrated a special gift to send me off to college.

You know what it was?

A pillowcase that had been screen printed with a cringy, posed picture of all those freshmen and sophomores standing at the front of the room. I was mortified.

I think the kids all thought it was cool. Maybe they even thought I would use it. I remember Mrs. T desperately trying to not start cracking up watching me open the gift. I realized in that moment she was fully aware of how little I cared about the underclassmen; that was the entire point.

I tried to fake a smile, but I just could not get over how embarrassing it was to get a pillowcase with a picture of a bunch of freshmen on it. They gave me a group hug just as the bell rang, but I just kept thinking, "These kids are SO LAME."

I remember walking out and Mrs. T waved and said, "See ya later Vincie!"

When report cards came home and I looked at my grade from Mrs. T, you know what I got?

An A+.

You know why?

Because I got all my work done and did a decent job. And just like all good high school teachers, Mrs. T graded me on my performance, not on how many friends I made. She really didn't care about that.

GOD'S REPORT CARD

A lot of us see our relationship with God this way. God is a teacher who only cares about our performance in obeying His commandments.

When it comes to how we treat the other Christians in our lives, we think that's not even part of the equation. As long as we're not outright mean, God is cool with us. In fact, maybe He even gives us a bit of applause for not needing any friendship or attention from the other Christians surrounding us at church.

Hear me say this.

God is not like Mrs. T.

Not at all.

Not one bit.

In the rest of this chapter, I hope to light the fire under your behind about the urgency to make good Christian friends. I hope to convince you that the time is now, and it's not that the tires of your life may pop.

It's that if you're flying solo, they've already popped, and you are already damaging your rims.

Here's why...and it's a reason that might surprise you.

I believe that the Bible teaches that there is a barrier between you and God if there is a barrier between you and God's people.

Let me say that another way.

If you are not close with God's family, God will not let you be close with Him.

DON'T GET STRUCK DEAD

I know that sounds crazy but let me explain by telling you the story of a husband and wife by the names of Ananias and Sapphira. This couple lived during the time when Jesus had already died, resurrected, and ascended into heaven, and the early church was in full swing.

During this time in church history, it was becoming common for wealthy people to sell everything they had and take all the money from their sales and give it to the church to help the poor.

And this was what Ananias and Sapphira did...well, sort of.

Acts 5:1-2 says this, *"Now a man named Ananias, together with his wife Sapphira, also sold a piece of property. With his wife's full knowledge he kept back part of the money for himself, but brought the rest and put it at the apostles' feet."*

Basically, Ananias and Sapphira sold some of their land. But instead of giving all of the money to the church, they kept some of the money for themselves and gave the rest to the church to help the poor.

Now, to be clear, this was **not** a sin. It was perfectly fine for Ananias and Sapphira to keep some of the money for themselves. And it was still a good thing to give the better part of the money to the church.

The problem came from the fact that Ananias made it seem as though the money he was giving to the church was the full amount he made from selling the land.

In other words, he was trying to **hide** what was going on **inside.**

He wanted the people around him to think he was being more generous than he really was. He wanted to put his best foot forward. He wanted to be seen like he had it all together, the perfect model Christian, when that just wasn't reality. So when he presents the money to Peter at the church, Peter confronts Ananias.

"Then Peter said, 'Ananias, how is it that Satan has so filled your heart that you have lied to the Holy Spirit and have kept for yourself some of the money you received for the land? Didn't it belong to you before it was sold? And after it was sold, wasn't the money at your disposal? What made you think of doing such a thing? You have not lied just to human beings but to God'" (Acts 5:3-4).

Peter was pointing out the issue in Ananias's heart.

He noticed the little white lie. He sensed a little bit of hypocrisy. He could see that Ananias didn't want to show other Christians what was really going on inside his heart. And Peter made it clear to Ananias that if he was hiding reality from other Christians, he was also lying to God.

Now, I bet you will never guess what happens next.

"When Ananias heard this, he fell down and died (Acts 5:5-6).

That's right. Ananias **drops dead.** Can you believe that? If you've ever thought the Bible was boring, think again. But the story gets worse. A few hours later, his wife Sapphira walks in and tells the same little lie.

And I know this sounds crazy, but when Peter confronts her, she also falls down dead.

HOW A HEAVENLY FATHER TREATS HIS EARTHLY CHILDREN

Now the point of this story is not, "Don't lie or God will strike you dead!"

I've seen a lot of Christians lie (myself included), and I haven't seen any of them get struck dead...yet (fingers crossed). Here's the point.

Because God is a loving parent, He is not okay with secrecy and hypocrisy among His children.

How open you are with your spiritual siblings matters deeply to your Heavenly Father.

Now, you might say, "I am confused.

I haven't lied to anyone.

I am NOT a hypocrite.

And why I haven't had time for Christian friends has nothing to do with not wanting to open up to other people!"

Here's what I would say in response to that.

Are you sure?

LET'S HAVE A MOMENT OF HONESTY

Let me tell you why most of us keep putting "Make friends with other Christians" at the bottom of our to-do lists.

We are just like Ananias and Sapphira.

We are scared for people to know the state of our hearts.

We don't want them to know our secret sins, struggles, temptations, and addictions.

We don't trust people enough to open up because we fear their judgment or disapproval.

We don't outright lie to anyone like Ananias and Sapphira.

No, no, no of course not. But here's what we do instead...

We don't make friends because we don't want friends to know how we're really doing.

If we keep people at a distance, hopefully, people will assume we have no issues.

We want to be seen as better than we are.

Do you know what the definition of hypocrisy is?

Wanting to be seen as better than we are.

We want to **hide** what's going on **inside.**

And God hates that heart posture, just as much as the outright lying that got Ananias and Sapphira struck dead.

That's not because God is harsh. It's actually because God is a loving parent.

God cares just as much about you being close with your spiritual siblings as you being close with Him.

EIGHT PEOPLE IN THREE BEDROOMS

I grew up in a big family. We had six kids crammed into a small three-bedroom house. Four boys and two girls. The girls were the bookends with four boys in the middle. No basement. Tiny yard. We were literally on top of each other.

The boys were pretty well-behaved when it came to how we treated our parents and sisters. But as brothers, we were often merciless with each other. I'm talking pushing, punching, hair pulling, and throwing every Star Wars plastic ray gun at one another. There were many bruises and bloody noses over the years.

Maybe we were extra violent, but maybe any group of four little boys were that way.

The worst fights were between me and Frankie. At one point, he knocked me unconscious. At another point, I remember squeezing his head so tightly that I was convinced his eyeballs were going to pop out. That was the plan at least.

I remember one of those fights ending with me looking squarely into my mom's eyes and saying, "I am never talking to Frankie again." And I meant it with ALL my heart.

Now, here's what my mom didn't say.

"Vincent, as long as you and I are getting along and as long as you're obeying me, I don't care if you never speak to Frankie again. All I care about is our relationship; I don't care about your relationship with your brother."

Looking back, I'm really glad my mom didn't have this mentality. And I would venture to say that no decent parent thinks that way. Why? Because good parents care about the whole family. They want to see their kids have great relationships with each other.

In fact, I have some memories of my parents even saying, "I don't care if you're mad at me, but you can't be mad at your siblings."

As long as I wouldn't talk to Frankie, my parents would be actively disciplining me.

As long as Frankie and I had a problem, me and my parents had a problem.

If there was distance between me and my siblings, there was distance between me and my parents.

DISTANCE PRODUCES MORE DISTANCE

Ananias and Sapphira wanted to KNOW God. They were showing up to every church service.

But Ananias and Sapphira didn't trust their spiritual brothers and sisters. They put on a good front, but they didn't want deep, close, vulnerable relationships.

And they were struck dead as a result.

Why?

Because God wants us to love Him, but He cares just as much (if not more) about how we love and treat each other.

Isn't that part of why in John 13:34 Jesus commanded us to *"love one another as I have loved you"*?

God is not okay with secrecy and hypocrisy among His children.

God's response to hypocrisy may not be striking us dead. I've never seen that since Acts 5. But what I have seen again and again and again are **Christians who find themselves distant and disconnected from other Christians and also feel distant and disconnected from God.**

And I do not believe that feeling distant from God is an illusion.

I believe that just like any loving parent, God will partially withhold Himself from you until you give yourself fully to a community. He still loves you. He still forgives you. But if you aren't willing to share your heart with your spiritual siblings, I don't know that God will fully share His heart with you.

If you don't ask for help from your spiritual siblings in the midst of struggle, I don't know that God will fully help you in your struggle.

God cares about you as your Heavenly Father, but as your Heavenly Father, He also puts high (and sometimes first) priority on your relationship with your spiritual siblings.

That's the bad news.

The flip side is the good news.

HOW TO GET CLOSER TO GOD

If you're willing to say yes to deep relationships with other Christians, I promise you'll find a deeper relationship with God.

When I was willing to be friends with my brother Frankie again, things immediately felt better between me and my parents. The two go hand in hand.

As you start to open up to your church, your small group, your pastor, and your friends about what's really going on, as you love them and let them love you, you will find a deeper, closer, more intimate connection with God. You'll start to sense His power all over your life.

If you're looking for the fastest way to change your life, you will need to start opening up to other Christians.

WHAT GETS THE ATTENTION OF A HURTING WORLD

To keep the good news train going, let me tell you why having strong Christian friendships impacts more lives than just your own.

Not only will you feel closer to God if you draw closer to your community, but you'll also show the people around you who don't know Jesus that God can change your life when you invest in relationships with other Christians.

Just to be blunt with you, those who are disconnected from God don't really care about how cool our church is or how much we do in the community.

That's generally all fluff in their minds.

The only thing that gets their attention is if we really love each other.

When we show up to small group and sing loud in church and participate on our outreach teams, the world notices.

When we confess our sins and pray for one another and encourage each other and challenge each other and make each other mad and make up and keep on loving each other, the world notices.

When we deliver casseroles when someone gets sick and show up in the hospital when someone gets cancer and cry at the funeral when someone dies and bring gifts to the baby shower when new life arrives, the world notices.

When we're all loving each other, the world wants to join in.

And so God's presence in our individual lives tends to show up based on the way we show up in community.

How are you showing up in Christian community?

GO

"I believe growing closer to God all boils down to this: if you are not serving, you will not be happy, and you will church-hop constantly. And if you are church-hopping, it is a lot harder to grow." - Dale Workman

9

Batteries Not Included

Following Jesus doesn't stop with just KNOWING and GROWING.

There are three pieces to this journey that Jesus takes His followers on.

The third piece is what I like to call the GO piece.

Jesus didn't just teach His followers how to have a personal relationship with God. And He didn't just teach them how to connect with each other. He sent them out to do the very same thing He was doing. He told them to GO make disciples and teach people how to follow Him. He sent them out to heal the sick, cast out demons, and transform cities.

When we GO, we are taking what we've learned in our relationship with God and from our Christian community and applying it so that we can tell other people about Jesus. We are using the gifts, talents, and abilities God has given us to grow His Kingdom, make a difference, and live out our purpose.

BATTERIES NOT INCLUDED

I have a fever dream memory from my childhood that I'm not even sure really happened. It is a memory of going to a random community theater production of some musical that was all about toys going on adventures together.

It wasn't Toy Story (this had to be 10 years before Woody and Buzz hit the theaters). I cannot find the musical no matter how hard I Google it. Maybe I dreamt it.

Who knows?

But there is a song in this fever dream of a toy car spinning in circles singing the line, "Batteries not included are the saddest words I know."

That line hit me hard as a kid.

And it stuck with me over the next 30 years.

At the time, my mind flashed to all the toys I had at home that had dead batteries (or no batteries) and were no longer lighting up and performing their various functions. I was filled with sadness as a result.

What if all those toys are secretly alive and living in the constant agony of a powerless life?

I had totally blown it.

Can you imagine being a toy car that couldn't turn its headlights on? What about my Star Wars blaster that had long since been robbed of its absurdly loud laser sounds? It must be horrible for them.

Obviously, life was not so terrible for my toys because they were not actually alive.

I have lived long enough to figure that out.

But I still feel the same sadness because I know as an adult that many of us are living in the horror of a seemingly powerless life.

Many of us feel like the batteries have not been included in our lives.

We feel that God has put a new season in front of us but hasn't given us the power to actually live it well.

Maybe you're looking at the challenges ahead in your faith, your recovery, a new job or lack of one, your relationships, your singleness, or your mental health, and you're thinking, "I do not have the power to face what's coming."

Where are the batteries, God? **I just feel too weak.**

If that's you today, I've got good news for you.

That power - the power that only comes from God - is available to you.

However, you're not going to receive that power the way you might think.

ROOM SHAKING POWER

Let me show you another moment from the Book of Acts involving Peter and John.

Peter and John just got thrown into prison for talking about Jesus. That could have been the end of the road for them, but they ended up being released from prison with a stern warning from the local authorities to no longer preach the good news. This was actually the first time that an official warning from the local government had been issued.

Once they got out of prison, Peter and John went back to their Christian friends and informed everyone that Christianity had just become illegal. This was a crucial moment when the early group of Jesus followers had to decide whether or not they were going to keep spreading the message.

Here's what happens next...

When they [the Christians] heard this, they raised their voices together in prayer to God. "Sovereign Lord," they said, "you made the heavens and the earth and the sea, and everything in them. You spoke by the Holy Spirit through the mouth of your servant, our father David:
"'Why do the nations rage
and the peoples plot in vain?

> *The kings of the earth rise up*
>   *and the rulers band together*
> *against the Lord*
>   *and against his anointed one.*
> *Indeed Herod and Pontius Pilate met together with the Gentiles and the people of Israel in this city to conspire against your holy servant Jesus, whom you anointed. They did what your power and will had decided beforehand should happen. Now, Lord, consider their threats and enable your servants to speak your word with great boldness. Stretch out your hand to heal and perform signs and wonders through the name of your holy servant Jesus"* (Acts 4:24-30).

In the face of incredible opposition, this rag-tag group decided that no matter the cost, they were going to stay committed to the purposes of God. They were going to continue to live their lives focused on the mission God had given them. They would do whatever it took to see more people meet Jesus.

Now, here's the cool part.

Watch how God responded to their **commitment** to His **purposes**.

After they prayed, the place where they were meeting was shaken. And they were all filled with the Holy Spirit and spoke the word of God boldly (Acts 4:31).

Don't miss this. In the face of opposition, they committed to the purpose God had for their lives. And how did God respond? The entire room started shaking!

Each one of them was filled with the Holy Spirit. They were so overcome with power that they all went out and faced the possibility of imprisonment or even death, seemingly without any fear.

What just happened?

God put some serious batteries into their lives.

DEAD BATTERIES

One of the greatest lies that we believe as Christians is that God has different types of power for different situations.

We believe He has *one* power available for our daily struggles.

And He has *another* type of power available for a greater purpose for our lives.

The reality is that **there is only one power source: the Holy Spirit.**

Have you ever thought about how modern cars have more battery-powered features than ever before to accommodate all our needs?

We've got instant heat and seat warmers for the winter. We've got A/C for the summer. Stereos that play our favorite playlists over Bluetooth. Some of the really fancy ones have little TVs in the back and the ever-coveted "CarPlay" in the front. Very swanky cars even have lane correction and rear-view cameras.

Now let me ask you this: If you park your car and turn off your engine, will all those features keep working?

Yes.

For a while.

But if the engine is off, all of the things inside your car that lead to a pleasant driving experience will continue to work, but the battery will also start to drain. Within a few hours at most, your battery will be dead, and all of those internal functions will no longer work.

However, as most of us know, if your engine is running and your car is moving, the battery will automatically recharge, and all of those nice internal features will run indefinitely.

The battery **stays charged** as the car moves forward.

And it is the **same battery** that powers all of the car's internal features that **meets our personal inside-the-car needs.**

KEEP YOUR BATTERIES CHARGED

This is how the Christian life works too.

God has given you a race to run, or to keep the metaphor going, a race to drive.

As you head toward God's purpose for your life, it is that very purpose that keeps your battery charged.

The same power from God that fuels our purpose is the same power that strengthens us for the daily struggles of life. If you try to use a car battery for the sole purpose of keeping you comfortable but don't actually drive, that battery will quickly run out.

In the same way, if you call on God's power to help you with your personal challenges, but never use any of that power to actually serve God's purposes in the world, that power quickly runs out.

The next sentence may be the most important in this book.

If you live your life for the good of others, for a greater purpose, God will give you the strength you need for your own challenges.

If you don't?

He won't.

The fastest way to change your life starts with living for the purposes of God.

If you are committed to the purposes of God, you'll receive the power of God.

If you are not committed to the purposes of God, you'll tend to not receive the power of God.

So if you want God's power, you're going to have to live for God's purposes.

WHAT KIND OF PURPOSE WILL BRING GOD'S POWER?

As you sit here and read that last statement, you might be confused about what it looks like to live for God's purposes.

Maybe you're thinking that you're already trying to say yes to God's purpose for your life.

That's why you gave your life to Jesus. Or that's why you rededicated your life to Jesus. And since you got serious about your faith, you've been reading your Bible and coming to church every week and praying every day. Maybe you even joined a small group! Isn't that you committing to God's purpose?

In a way, yes!

But also, no.

Let me try to bring some clarity to this question.

There are different types of commitment.

There is a commitment to doing the basics of Christianity: coming to church, reading your Bible, praying, etc.

That kind of commitment is great, but it's not the kind of commitment that draws the room-shaking empowerment of God.

God didn't just create you to commit to Christian-type things that help you grow personally. That stuff is all good. BUT you were created to serve the purposes of God in the world. You were made to introduce people to Jesus, to serve people in need, to make the world a better place, and to love those who are difficult to love. You are here to be an ambassador for Christ in the world around you. God has good works prepared in advance for you to do (Eph 2:10).

As you start to say yes to doing things like these, things that don't directly benefit yourself, things that build God's kingdom, that's like a car actually driving. It's how God recharges your battery. When you say yes to the purposes of God, He says yes to His power.

That same power that keeps your God-given purpose moving forward is also the power that gives you strength for all the other day-to-day aspects of life.

The power for all the challenges you face at home, at work, in relationships, and in your finances, that power flows from the same battery that empowers your purpose.

Like I said before, if you want to experience the power of God, you are going to have to commit to the purposes of God.

THE PURSUIT OF HAPPINESS

Now maybe you're reading this, and you immediately get it.

And you are READY to do something that makes a difference in the world.

Or maybe...the opposite is true.

You just don't feel a strong desire to find a greater purpose for your life.

I get that. I think a lot of us are so stuck in survival mode that making a difference in the world seems like a very unreal desire. We're all just trying to find happiness in our day-to-day lives.

A lot of people say, "Humans just want to be happy."

I've even heard some theologians say that happiness and pleasure are the deepest desires in our fleshly, selfish human hearts.

We want to scroll on Instagram until our brains fall out.

We want to online shop until we drop.

We want to work where we want, spend time with who we want, love who we want, sleep with who we want, and as long as we're happy, that's all that matters.

It's easy to assume that if the only way we're going to receive greater power from God is to find a greater purpose for our lives, then most of us might as well give up and just live powerless lives.

Call me overly optimistic, but I don't think that's true.

Despite the damage our souls have received from being born into a sinful and broken world, I think there is far more to the human spirit than just living for the next little dopamine hit.

WE ALL WANT TO FIGHT FOR SOMETHING

Think about it.

In times of war, people who are **not** following Jesus volunteer to serve in the military and give their lives to protect their country. If all those people cared about was their own happiness, they wouldn't voluntarily enlist in the military.

They enlist because they want their life to count for something. They want to help make someone else's life better.

Similarly, if all people cared about was their own happiness, why would anyone have children?

That's (kind of) a joke.

But if you are a parent, or you know a parent, then you know having kids is HARD WORK!

It's exhausting. It's tear-inducing. It means dying to yourself constantly. But people, Christian or not, have kids all the time.

Why? Because people want to do something that matters, even if it doesn't make them happier all the time.

And if you are a Christian, hear me say this.

I firmly believe **your** desire for purpose is deeper than your desire for happiness. Even though your flesh may say, "I just want to be happy," the Holy Spirit within you gives you the desire to make a difference and live out your purpose to build God's Kingdom.

There is something deep in you that wants to fight for something good and beautiful.

And from that desire to live with purpose comes the opportunity for you to experience God's power like never before.

As you find the power to start to live for a greater purpose in your life, you will also find the power to overcome your day-to-day struggles.

The power you need to save your failing marriage comes from living out your God-given purpose.

The power you need to mend your relationship with your kids comes from living out your God-given purpose.

The power you need to resist the temptation of sexual sin comes from living out your God-given purpose.

The power you need to overcome your addiction comes from living out your God-given purpose.

The power you need to stay hopeful in the midst of a heartbreaking diagnosis comes from living out your God-given purpose.

So what does that look like for you specifically?

Well, we're going to do a whole chapter on how to find your purpose. But let me say briefly that finding your purpose is a process.

Maybe for you, living out your purpose starts with simply serving as a greeter at church.

Or maybe it's serving in the kids' ministry and teaching children about Jesus.

Or maybe it's volunteering in student ministry and mentoring middle school and high school students.

Or maybe it's becoming a pastor or serving as a missionary or starting a non-profit.

There are so many opportunities for you to use your talents, your time, and your testimony to build God's kingdom and live out His purpose for your life.

So whatever that looks like for you, I want to encourage you to take one step into that purpose today.

Say yes to commitment to God's purpose. Because I can promise you that when you do, you'll experience the fullness of God's power.

"Living out my calling as a youth pastor is one of the most fulfilling journeys I've ever experienced. There's nothing like seeing students' lives transformed by the love of Jesus and knowing I get to play a part in their stories. It reminds me every day that serving others is not just something I'm supposed to do but something I get to do." - Kevin Cave

10

How To Find Your Calling

In the last chapter, we talked about the fact that if you want the power of God in your life, you're going to need to commit yourself to the purposes of God in the world.

In this chapter, we're going to double-click on that idea.

Let's get personal when it comes to the GO part of KNOW, GROW, and GO.

One of the most life-changing things you will ever do is find your calling.

To prove it to you, I'm going to talk about bicycles (again).

When you're riding a bicycle, how do you make sure the bike stays upright? By pedaling it and moving it forward, right?

The more a bicycle slows down, the more it starts to wobble and the harder it is to keep the bicycle from toppling over. Unless you're a professional BMX rider, I don't care if you've been riding a bike for 30+ years.

You're going to fall over if the bike is going really slow.

Our life change works the same way.

When you've got a sense of calling in your life, when you're moving forward with intention, purpose, and speed toward doing something for God, it's like you've got momentum, direction, and energy. You're moving forward at a good pace, and the bicycle of your life stays upright.

You've got the purpose you need to not fall back into old habits, patterns, and tendencies.

On the other hand, when you've got no purpose, direction, or momentum, when you're living for yourself, when you feel like you don't have a calling, you start to move slower and slower, and it becomes easier and easier to fall back into old, unhealthy habits and behaviors.

The fastest way to change your life involves finding your life's calling.

One of the saddest things is when people can't find their calling, and I don't want that to be your story.

WHY WE DON'T FIND OUR CALLING

There are two main reasons we don't find our calling.

Reason 1: We overly glamorize it.

We expect to find a calling that's going to sound easy, exciting, and fulfilling. We think our calling will use all of our gifts and talents and will always be enjoyable. So if we can't think of anything like that off the top of our heads, we "can't find our calling."

It's kind of like that old saying that goes, "Find a job you love, and you'll never work a day in your life." We often apply the same logic and think, "Find a calling you love, and you'll never have a meaningless day in your life."

Don't get me wrong, your calling will add value and meaning to your life.

But starting with the perspective of "What sounds cool?" is actually the wrong starting place.

Reason 2: We assume our <u>career</u> is our <u>calling</u>.

The second reason people miss their calling is that they just take whatever they're currently doing for work and rename it their calling.

It sounds something like this.

I want to be a plumber, so I'll be a plumber for Jesus. I'll be really kind to my customers, and I'll do business in an honest way.

I want to be a lawyer, so I'll be a lawyer for Jesus. I won't bend or break any laws, and I'll work with the utmost integrity.

I want to be a teacher, so I'll be a teacher for Jesus. I'll be kind and compassionate towards my students, and I'll be an example to them.

These are all great things, and God definitely receives glory when you do your job this way.

The Bible is very clear that whether we eat or drink or do whatever (1 Corinthians 10:31) we should do it for God's glory. But I would venture to say that working hard and doing your best at a 9-5 job that you love is still not what it means to find your calling in this world.

But if we assume that it's good enough to just have a career that we go about in a God-glorifying way, we are not connected to the Biblical definition of calling.

WHAT A CALLING REALLY LOOKS LIKE

The truth is, our calling often begins by doing things for God that we don't really want to do.

To show you what I mean, let's look at the life of Paul from Acts 18. In just these few short paragraphs, we see Paul living out the calling God has given him. Paul is known as one of the greatest evangelists in all of history, but we see from the following passage of Scripture that even his calling wasn't as glamorous as you might expect.

"and because he [Paul] was a tentmaker as they were, he stayed and worked with them. Every Sabbath he reasoned in the synagogue, trying to persuade Jews and Greeks.

When Silas and Timothy came from Macedonia, Paul devoted himself exclusively to preaching, testifying to the Jews that Jesus was the Messiah. But when they opposed Paul and became abusive, he shook out his clothes in protest and said to them, "Your blood be on your own heads! I am innocent of it. From now on I will go to the Gentiles."

Then Paul left the synagogue and went next door to the house of Titius Justus, a worshiper of God. Crispus, the synagogue leader, and his entire household believed in the Lord; and many of the Corinthians who heard Paul believed and were baptized.

One night the Lord spoke to Paul in a vision: "Do not be afraid; keep on speaking, do not be silent. For I am with you, and no one is going to attack and harm you, because I have many people in this city." So Paul stayed in Corinth for a year and a half, teaching them the word of God (Acts 18:3-11).

Let's recap this passage.

For starters, Paul has to work a second job as a tentmaker to pay the bills (Acts 18:3). He endures some heavy verbal abuse from those he's trying to minister to (Acts 18:5-6). And Paul is, on some level, afraid because we see God encourage him not to fear (Acts 18:9-11).

Paul had an incredible calling on his life to preach the good news of Jesus to people everywhere he went, but this calling didn't come without its share of challenges.

When God puts a calling on your life, sometimes that means you have very difficult tasks and circumstances ahead that come as a result of your calling.

It also means that the calling God gives you will likely feel...

- big and scary and overwhelming
- too much to handle
- impossible to live out

That's all just part of the deal.

Because the reality is, whatever God calls you to do is going to be big for you.

If it doesn't feel big, it's not God's calling.

But, on a more encouraging note, Paul's calling is what he refers to as THE motivating factor in his life to keep going, to keep pressing on even when life gets hard (2 Corinthians 4:1). In a nutshell, Paul said, "Because I have this calling, I do not give up."

So while we are often looking for a calling that is easy and life-giving, the reality is that many people who find their calling would say that it is very difficult, very challenging, and very painful.

Once we accept this reality, we're going to be one step closer to finding the calling the Lord has in store for us.

So how do we actually find it?

WHAT DOES GOD VALUE?

Back in the day, I worked as a server at a local restaurant. The longer I worked there, the more I saw my server friends start getting promoted to become shift leaders and managers. Naturally, as I saw them move up the ladder, I wanted the same to happen for me. So one day, I approached my boss and asked for a promotion.

Before I continue this story, one very important detail you need to be aware of is that I was a HORRIBLE server. I was constantly making mistakes. I was disorganized. I wouldn't write things down. I didn't even memorize the menu. I was basically doing the bare minimum to get by at this job.

Thankfully, when I approached my boss about getting promoted, he was very kind and non-judgmental towards me, despite my status as one of the worst servers he had at the restaurant. But he was still honest with me. He essentially told me that if I wanted to get promoted, I had to start caring about the things he cared about.

That meant I would need to learn the menu. I would need to be more organized so I could get to my tables faster. I would need to write everything down and make fewer mistakes. If that promotion was going to happen, I was going to need to value what my boss valued.

As much as I may already be making you less excited to find your calling than you were when the chapter started, let me make it even a little less appealing.

The way we start to find our calling is by abandoning our values in favor of God's values.

If you really want to figure out what your calling is, you can't start by asking...

"What is life-giving to me?"

You have to start by asking...

"What does God value?"

Sometimes we want a significant calling, but we don't really care about what God cares about deeply.

Finding your calling means caring about the things God cares about and valuing the things He values.

THE TRIANGLE OF CALLING

Now, if you're staring at this page and asking, "Well Vince, are you going to tell me what God cares about?" Yes, I am. And to do that, I want to introduce you to the Triangle of Calling.

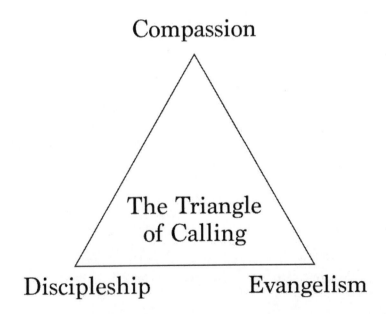

This triangle is made up of the three things God cares about: Evangelism, Discipleship, and Compassion.

To put it simply, your calling is found in doing something that moves the needle on one, two, or all three of these things.

And for many of us, doing these three things is **not** going to be found in our careers.

Remember, Paul was a tentmaker, and he glorified God with that career, but that was not his calling. He had a calling outside of his career that involved the triangle.

When you start to do something in the triangle, you will start to find your calling. That might be...
- Inviting friends to church (Evangelism)
- Volunteering at a homeless shelter (Compassion)
- Going on a mission trip (Evangelism)
- Leading a small group (Discipleship)
- Sponsoring a child overseas (Compassion)
- Serving on a volunteer team at your church (Any of the above)

This is just a list to get you started.

There are hundreds of ways you can live out your calling.

The important thing is that you're caring about what God cares about, and you're valuing what He values.

LEGOS AND PERIOD DRAMAS

Now, I do want to acknowledge the fact that the examples I listed above aren't always easy or enjoyable. They can be difficult. They can involve awkward or hard conversations. They can be inconvenient and sometimes even draining for you. And those are characteristics we wouldn't expect to be true of our calling.

But I want you to realize that living out your calling changes your life not because it's necessarily enjoyable, but because God moves towards you when you move towards the things He loves.

My wife Joanna does not love Legos in the slightest.

But when we go to Target, we often linger in the Lego section, and I show her all the Legos I'm into. She takes an interest in what I'm interested in, and I am filled with warmth towards her.

In the same way, I don't love period dramas. To be honest, I find them quite boring (probably the same way Joanna finds Legos to be boring.) But Joanna loves period dramas, so I watch them with her because she's interested in them. And when I take an interest in her interests, she is filled with warmth towards me.

It's okay if you looked at the calling triangle and thought, "I'm just not that excited about evangelism, or discipleship, or compassion…"

If that's true of you, but you still choose to show interest in what God is interested in, He moves towards you when you value what He values.

When it comes to being a pastor, there are a lot of weeks when I'm not excited about preaching on a Sunday morning. Or there are meetings I'm not excited to lead. But I engage in these things because I believe they are things God is interested in, and they move the needle on evangelism, discipleship, and compassion. When I do these things and live out my calling, I feel closer to God, and I believe God moves towards me.

THE HELPER'S HIGH

Okay, after several pages of talking about how hard and painful it can be to live out your calling, let's get positive (for at least a few minutes).

When you do something unpleasant, uncomfortable, or painful for the benefit of others, there is an IMMEDIATE benefit to you.

If you are feeling spiritually unhealthy (depressed, anxious, lethargic, apathetic, self-loathing, or whatever else), part of the reason may be because you are not getting regular spiritual exercise.

A secret ingredient to getting spiritually healthy is doing something good for someone else.

Even non-Christian social scientists have stumbled upon the same discovery.

A dude named Allan Luks wrote a book called "The Healing Power of Doing Good: The Health and Spiritual Benefits of Helping Others" in which he coined a phrase that has haunted me on a regular basis: "The Helper's High."

The Helper's High is a measurable spike in endorphins, dopamine, and oxytocin that occurs when people do something for someone other than themselves.

Don't miss that.

If you live for yourself, your brain is actually producing fewer chemicals that make you feel happy.

Sure, there might be plenty of other reasons you feel low.

But don't rule out the possibility that part of the reason you're down is because your life has been all about you.

THE PINNACLE OF FLOURISHING

Another researcher, Abraham Maslow, created a pyramid of human flourishing, essentially arguing that a fulfilled human being needs the following things in the following order to be fulfilled.

The list originally went as follows:
1. Food, clothing, and shelter
2. Safety from danger
3. Love and belonging
4. Respect from others
5. Self-actualization (or personal growth)

Decades after this pyramid was published and popularized, Maslow told the world he got it partially wrong.

As an aging man, he claimed that his original viewpoint actually lacked a sixth level, the very pinnacle of human existence.

He called this final level of fulfillment "transcendence."

Simply put, transcendence was the experience of giving your life away to a cause greater than yourself.

Let me ask you...do you care about transcendence?

Do you want to give your life away for something bigger than yourself?

Or do you want to settle for a life that is lived solely focused on you?

PURPOSE IS A SWEATY BUSINESS

Earlier in my ministry days, I served in a youth group in a very affluent church. The students in this youth group came from wealthy families, and their lifestyle made that quite clear. They all drove fancy cars. They wore nice clothes, and they had every expensive gadget on the market.

Needless to say, they lived very comfortable lives.

Every year, we would take 30-40 of these students on an overseas mission trip to serve in a community that operated under very humble conditions, a far cry from what these students were used to.

Most of the students would sign up for this trip just for the sense of adventure. They glamorized it. The male students showed up hoping to flirt with the female students. The female students showed up wearing their best adventure gear and a full face of makeup.

It looked like they were going on a spring break trip to Europe instead of a mission trip to a third-world country.

But every single year, without fail, all of their selfish motivations dissolved within 24 hours of being on the mission field.

These students would learn quickly that these trips required blood, sweat, and tears. They would build houses. They would put on VBS in 100+ degree temperatures. They would do whatever was asked of them, and that included accepting the living conditions of whatever country we were in.

We would sometimes stay with the local families during these trips, which included eating local, sometimes questionable food and sleeping in homes that were made of scraps and scrounged-up materials. I even remember one year, one of our female students was sleeping in a bed and the family's dog climbed in the bed with her and peed in the bed. She slept there, in the dog pee, crying, for the rest of the night.

It was always obvious the first couple of days that the students hated it.

But as the week progressed, they started to fall in love with the things that God loved, and everything started to change.

At the end of the week, everyone returned home looking dirty and disheveled.

But they also came back on fire for Jesus because they had learned to value what He values.

They came back sweaty, they came back fulfilled, and they came back having fallen in love with a new sense of calling.

They had told people about the gospel for the very first time.

With love and compassion, they served these people who were much less fortunate than them.

They came back changed...pedaling their metaphorical bicycle faster than ever.

They had learned what it looked like to love what Jesus loved.

They had found their calling...or at least the substance of it.

And they were excited to come back and live out their calling the way they had on that mission trip.

The same is true for us when we do the things God wants us to do - as difficult as they are, as out of our comfort zone as they are, as non-life-giving as they sometimes are - when we care about what God cares about and value what He values, that's how we will begin to live out our calling and experience all of the joy, purpose, and momentum that comes with it.

"I feel closer to the Lord when I serve. I know I am doing what He has asked us to do, and I can tell it makes a difference. I know more people at the church, and I feel almost an ownership of the church. Maybe like I have skin in the game? Whatever it is, what God is doing at The Bridge seems so much more personal to me because I am serving there too." - Shandon Stamper

11

The Purpose Plop

Have you ever had one of those friends who wants to get married but refuses to do a single stitch of work to find a partner?

We've all known someone like that. One of their deepest desires in life is to have a spouse and a family. But then they mention how discouraged they've felt lately because there has been little to no progress in their dating life.

You smile empathetically, and you decide to ask your friend some questions in hopes of maybe helping them get a little closer to seeing their hopes become a reality.

"Well, what are you doing to give yourself the opportunity to meet someone?"

"What do you mean?" your friend asks, seemingly puzzled.

So you respond, "Are you spending time in environments that would allow you to meet new people?"

"Well, not really. I like to hang out with just my close group of friends," your friend says.

"Okay then. Are you involved at your church where you could possibly meet someone else who's involved?" You ask hopefully.

"I mean, I go to church most weeks. But I usually get there right when the service starts. I sit in the back, and then I leave right after the message."

"Alright. Well, have you told your close friends you're willing to be set up with people they know who might be a good match?" You're starting to run out of ideas.

"No, I haven't. I'm not really comfortable with blind dates," your friend admits.

At this point you're frustrated. So you decide to ask one more question. You say, "So, how exactly are you planning on meeting someone to date then?" The irritation in your voice is likely noticeable.

And in the most nonchalant tone, your friend responds, "Oh that's easy! I'm just waiting for God to bring them into my life."

This is the part of the hypothetical story where you probably have quite a flabbergasted look on your face.

At this point, my response would be "Well, I hope you're okay with marrying your Amazon delivery person. Because that is now your only option."

If you want to be married, you can't just sit around and wait for God to plop your spouse on your front doorstep.

And while that might seem like an obvious reality when it comes to dating, many Christians are going through life having similar expectations surrounding their purpose.

The reason why so few people actually end up having a purpose for their lives is because most people expect their purpose to plop into their lap like an Amazon-air-dropped package from heaven.

They **want** to live out their purpose. They **want** to fulfill their God-given destiny. But they are going about their lives expecting God to plop their purpose in their lap without putting in any effort of their own.

It's like one day, they want to just wake up and be able to say,

"Plop! I just led someone into a relationship with Jesus."
"Plop! I just became a small group leader."
"Plop! I just started investing in students in the youth group."
"Plop! I just launched a non-profit."

That's not how it works.

For the next few pages, I want to give you a simple guide to finding your purpose as demonstrated by the life of a guy named Philip.

PHILIP'S STORY

Now, you might remember Philip from our discussion in Chapter 3 about Simon the Sorcerer.

At that time, Philip was in full swing of walking in his God-given purpose. Philip was actually leading a movement of God so big that the Bible tells us the entire city where he was ministering was filled with joy (Acts 8:8).

But what you may not know is that Philip's life didn't always look like that. Before Philip started preaching the gospel and performing miracles by the power of the Holy Spirit, the manifestation of Philip's purpose looked quite different, which is exactly what we're going to see as we dive into Acts chapter 6.

At this time in history, the church took on the responsibility of feeding the widows in the community. There was no way for widows to financially provide for themselves, so the members of the church would make sure the widows had enough food to eat.

The problem was that some of the widows were getting overlooked.

So the apostles met to talk about this issue and tried to figure out what they needed to do to make sure none of these widows went without food.

"So the Twelve gathered all the disciples together and said, 'It would not be right for us to neglect the ministry of the word of God in order to wait on tables. Brothers and sisters, choose seven men from among you who are known to be full of the Spirit and wisdom. We will turn this responsibility over to them and will give our attention to prayer and the ministry of the word'" (Acts 6:2-4).

Now, one thing to note.

I realize this sounds kind of harsh when the disciples are saying it would not be right for them "to wait tables." It honestly sounds a little snobby at first glance. But I don't believe that was their heart at all. Instead, I think they were genuinely wanting to find people who could serve these widows so that the disciples could keep preaching and not be stretched too thin.

So with this heart posture, they selected seven men to be members of a team to bring food to the widows. Once the team was selected, the disciples prayed over these men. They commissioned them. And they sent them off to begin serving.

"This proposal pleased the whole group. They chose Stephen, a man full of faith and of the Holy Spirit; also Philip, Procorus, Nicanor, Timon, Parmenas, and Nicolas from Antioch, a convert to Judaism. They presented these men to the apostles, who prayed and laid their hands on them" (Acts 6:5-6).

Did you notice whose name was mentioned as part of this team?

Philip!

Philip was a member of the food delivery team.

Philip's purpose didn't just plop in his lap out of nowhere.

There was a process to get there.

And that process didn't start with deliverance and miracles.

It started with delivering meals.

Philip may have felt the call on his life to bring revival. But that's not where God started with him. The Lord had a different beginning in mind...which shows us an important truth when it comes to our purpose.

How did Philip make the transition from the food team to the joy-for-a-whole-city team?

Well, that is a much longer and more complicated story, but trust me, he didn't engineer it. Philip just kept being obedient to God; he kept moving forward and doing the next purposeful thing in front of him, and God kept opening the doors until Philip landed in the right place.

THE PROCESS OF PURPOSE

Here's the point.

Every purpose requires a process.

This process takes time.

It takes small steps of obedience.

It takes faithfulness in the seemingly insignificant moments.

But it's in these small steps and moments of unseen faithfulness that begin your process toward fulfilling the purpose God has for your life.

Here's what I want to challenge you with, and it is a horrible parody of the Nike slogan.

Just do something.

I don't care what it is.

Don't wait for the right thing, just do something.

STEERING PARKED CARS

Have you ever had to make a hard left turn into a parking spot, but then back out in the opposite direction? If it's hard to visualize what I just said, picture being parked and having to turn your wheels from all the way left to all the way right without the car being in motion. Isn't that such a painful experience? You can hear your tires squeaking and squawking. You're worried the people surrounding you think it's your first time driving.

And you know what else?

Turning the wheels doesn't actually turn your car.

You can't change the actual direction of a car unless the car is moving.

If you sit in a parked car and turn your wheels all the way to the left and then all the way to the right, you will not actually have moved the position of the vehicle itself even one centimeter.

Our lives work the same way.

If you sit and think, "Should I do x or y? Should I go to the left or the right? Should I go to this church or that church? Should I serve on this team or that one? Should I go here or there?" it's like you're turning your tires back and forth and creating a horrible racket, but not accomplishing anything.

But if you start driving your car, then even the slightest movement of the steering wheel will change your direction.

When it comes to your purpose:

- Your responsibility is the gas pedal
- God's responsibility is the steering wheel

If you will just start moving,
God will start steering.

The fastest way to change your life requires finding some small way to change someone else's.

That's what happened with Philip, isn't it? He started out delivering food and God brought him to a place of bringing revival to an entire city.

HOW I FOUND MY CALLING

This is my story as well.

I am currently a pastor at a church that has seen countless salvations, baptisms, and lives changed. Being a pastor is not the ultimate purpose; it's just the one God had for me.

But I didn't just wake up one day as a pastor.

I started out volunteering as a worship leader singing way off-key for a youth group of just a handful of students back when I was 16.

Here's a quick outline of my life's events:

- Whiny teen worship leader
- Whiny twenty-something worship leader
- Very stressed seminary student
- Confused production director
- Unqualified kids pastor
- Unexpected executive pastor
- Overwhelmed lead pastor

It took me almost two full decades to go from whiney worship leader to pastor of a growing, high-impact church. And God had to guide me every step of the way. I had no clue where I was going at the beginning, but all I knew was to just keep saying yes.

God has a way of steering you in the right direction if you are just willing to press the gas pedal.

PEDAL TO THE METAL

That being said, here's my challenge to you:

Just do something for God.

Hold the door open when the person is way too far away, and you feel awkward standing there.

Serve in the nursery at your church.

Volunteer at a homeless shelter.

Help an old lady across the street.

Jump someone's car.

Take out $20 at an ATM and give it to a stranger.

I don't care.

I don't think God does either.

Just start moving, and He'll start steering.

THREE TYPES OF FUNERALS

Now, I know that there are going to be days when finding your purpose can easily slip to the bottom of your priority list. In the midst of all the stresses of life, we often don't feel any urgency to make a difference in other people's lives.

But the reality is, though it may not feel crucial today, your purpose will be what defines the whole story of your life.

Nobody likes to think about this, but there is going to be a funeral for you with real people in attendance one day. And one of the biggest defining factors of what is said at that funeral will be whether or not your life had any purpose beyond you, your friends, your career, and your immediate family.

To put it simply, how you live your life now determines how you're remembered later.

As a pastor, I have attended a number of funerals. Some have hundreds of people in attendance, others only a handful. But without fail, when it comes to recounting someone's life, it's painfully obvious what kind of life they lived.

There are essentially three types of funerals.

The first is the funeral of a downright hated person. Those are the saddest, and also fairly rare.

The second type is the funeral of the person who lived the basic American dream type life. At these funerals, you'll hear things like:

...Loving husband.

...Caring mother.

...Hardworking individual.

...Always nice to everyone.

Everyone around the room tries to plaster on their face the ideal concoction of empathy and admiration. But the vibe is obvious. Everyone is kinda freaking out with the horrible realization that the deceased did everything you're "supposed to do," and it all amounted to nothing.

The person whose body is in the casket basically lived for the benefit of themselves and their immediate family.

They essentially made no difference in the world outside of their own interests and comforts.

They were a decent parent and partner and passed out of this world with a few dollars in the bank. But they will not be remembered for more than a few months except by the handful closest to them.

Now don't get me wrong, this second type of funeral is better than the first.

Being a good husband or wife or parent or provider are all great goals. I believe they're the foundation of a life well lived. But it seems that so many people build the foundation of a good life but stop there and never actually build a house or apartment or even a tiny little shack of a greater purpose on that foundation.

But then there is a third type of funeral.

And these funerals are the best.

The third type is the funeral of the person who built a foundation but didn't stop there. You hear things like...

Dedicated their life to providing for the needy.

Invested countless hours in the next generation.

Tirelessly worked to care for the hurting in our community.

A spiritual mother or father to many.

Showed us what it looks like to live sacrificially.

Will be remembered by many for a long, long time.

I hope that my funeral is the third type.

Don't you want yours to be the third type too?

CONCLUSION

12

Now What?

If you want your life to change, you need to become a different person than you are today.

And as we've discussed throughout this book, the fastest way to become that kind of person is to KNOW, GROW, and GO.

Now, you might be thinking, "That might change my life, but that sounds like a lot of work."

If that's you right now, I want you to know that I get it. However, eating healthy, drinking water, and exercising is **also** a lot of work.

But whether you like it or not, that's the work it takes to become physically healthy. It's what your body is wired for, and there's no way to feel good physically without those three things.

In the same way, there is no way to be spiritually healthy without KNOWING, GROWING, and GOING. It's simply what you're wired for spiritually.

But here's the good news.

Even though it's a lot of work, I can assure you that you will come to crave it.

YOU WILL CRAVE KNOWING, GROWING, AND GOING

I didn't start drinking coffee until I was 25 years old.

I know, I know. How did I survive? Honestly, I have no clue. But I discovered the glory that is coffee at age 25.

At the time, I was working for a church that was a setup and teardown church, which meant every Sunday, I showed up at 6am to help the team set up church at a Bollywood movie theater and would then stay late after service to tear everything down.

Obviously, this was a pretty tiring gig, so I started drinking coffee on Sunday mornings to see if the caffeine would help boost my energy. And boy did that magical bean juice make a HUGE difference. So now, I don't just drink coffee on Sundays. I drink coffee every single day.

To be honest, when I first started drinking it, I didn't really like the taste of it.

But I liked the way it made me feel, and I loved the energy it gave me, so I began to crave coffee every morning.

Now, before I ever experienced the power of coffee, if someone had come up to me and tried to sell me on making my own coffee at home - buying a coffee maker, buying coffee grounds, learning the right coffee-to-water ratio, buying and switching out filters, getting all the cream and sugar I needed to add - I would have had no interest because it sounded like a lot of work and effort just for a cup of coffee.

But, once I experienced its power and saw the difference it made in my life, I very quickly bought all the things and did all the steps to make sure I had coffee in my kitchen every single morning.

What once sounded like too much work has now become something I crave.

The same is true for KNOWING, GROWING, and GOING.

It feels like a lot of work on the front end.

It feels like a lot of work to show up to church each week and to wake up early to read your Bible — KNOWING God.

It feels like a lot of work to get a group of friends who will hold you accountable in your faith and who can follow Jesus with you — GROWING in Christian community.

It feels like a lot of work to serve and do something with your gifts and talents to make an impact — GOING to make a difference.

It all feels like a lot of work, but as you start to practice these things, as you start to feel the power of KNOWING, GROWING, and GOING, and as your life starts to change, you will start to crave what once felt like too much work.

THE FASTEST WAY IS DOING ALL THREE

Now that you have a better understanding of what it means to KNOW, GROW, and GO, you might be thinking about the most common questions I get asked when I start telling someone about KNOW, GROW, and GO:

What if I just do one of the three?

Or what if I just do two of the three?

Isn't that enough for my life to change?

While these seem like fair questions – after all, doing one or two is definitely better than doing zero – I can't stress enough how important it is to do ALL THREE if you want to experience quick and radical life change.

Let's go back, once again, to our metaphor of eating healthy, drinking water, and exercising.

If you choose to just do one or two of those, you're definitely going to feel better than if you aren't doing any of them.

If you go from eating junk food to eating healthy, you're going to feel better. But if you're eating healthy while not drinking any water or exercising, you're still not going to feel great.

If you're drinking enough water, but you're not eating healthy or exercising, you're going to feel weak and exhausted.

If you're exercising but you're not eating healthy foods or drinking enough water, you're not going to make a lot of progress.

Only when you do all three things - eat healthy, drink water, and exercise - will you start to notice a change in your health and feel better.

The same is true with KNOWING, GROWING, and GOING.

If you want to experience a fast and noticeable change in your spiritual life, you have to do all three.

If you're still skeptical, let me paint a picture of what your life could look like if you choose to only do one or two of the KNOW, GROW, and GO steps.

IF YOU ONLY KNOW GOD

Maybe you'd say, "I'm only going to KNOW God. I'm just going to come to church, read my Bible, and pray. That's it."

Guess what? If that's all you do, you're going to feel pumped up on Sunday morning, but that fire will fade by Sunday night. You're going to be reading your Bible and praying, but you're going to feel lonely, isolated, disconnected, and purposeless. It's going to be better than nothing, but it's not going to allow you to experience the change you're hoping for.

Then, after a while, you'll likely become very bored of Sunday morning. You'll end up skipping the sermon series that "doesn't apply to you." You'll get annoyed when you hear some of the same worship songs on repeat. You become very focused on what you consume, and you don't focus on how you can contribute. This is bound to happen at some point in your walk with Jesus. But it's how you lean in and persevere when this starts to happen that's important.

IF YOU ONLY KNOW & GROW

Or maybe you'd say, "I'm going to KNOW and GROW. I'm going to invest in my relationship with God and join a small group. But that's all."

Again, while that's better than nothing, you're still going to feel like you have no purpose. You're going to feel apathetic towards others. You're going to feel selfish, and your group will probably have trouble getting along because there's no greater purpose to tie you together if your group isn't doing anything together for the Kingdom of God.

IF YOU ONLY KNOW & GO

Or maybe you'd say, I'm going to KNOW and GO. I'm going to know God better and I'm going to serve on a team in my church. But that's it."

Sure, you're going to feel like you have purpose and you're going to feel closer to God, but no one is going to know what's really going on in your life. You're going to be carrying around all these secrets because you have no one to share them with, and those secrets are going to make you sick.

IF YOU ONLY GROW & GO

And then if you decide to only GROW and GO, you're not going to feel connected to God. You're going to feel spiritually dry and distant. And you're going to stay stuck, unable to make any spiritual progress because you're not getting to know God better or investing in your relationship with Him.

Do you see what I mean?

If you really want your life to be different, you have to implement ALL THREE steps - KNOW, GROW, **and** GO.

IF YOU KNOW, GROW, AND GO

So, what will your life look like if you KNOW, GROW, and GO? I'm glad you asked.

If you start living out all three of these steps consistently and simultaneously, I believe your life is going to change in a big way.

You're going to watch God bring redemption to your broken marriage.

You're going to cultivate stronger and healthier relationships with your kids while you grow as a parent.

You're going to experience the love of Christian community when your small group rallies around you in the midst of your pain and heartbreak.

You're going to gain friends who hold you accountable and help you quit drinking, quit smoking, or quit looking at pornography.

You're going to find freedom from your anger problem that's been holding you back and hurting your relationships because you learn to confess and receive prayer from other Christians.

You're going to find strength from God to overcome your most difficult struggles.

You're going to discover your purpose and begin to impact other people around you as you live out that God-given purpose.

You're going to be an unrecognizable version of yourself...all because you chose to KNOW, GROW, and GO.

GIVE IT TIME

Now, I want to take a minute to talk to the person who is currently KNOWING, GROWING, and GOING, but they feel like it's not working.

If that's where you are today, trust me, I get it. It's totally possible to feel like you're doing all the right things but nothing seems to be changing. But I want to give you some encouragement so you don't have to stay stuck in that place.

If you're investing in your relationship with God, you're in a small group, and you're serving, but you feel like change isn't happening, let me give you two challenges:

First, I want you to give it time. If it's only been a week or two that you've been KNOWING, GROWING, and GOING, don't expect everything to change that quickly. Just like with our physical health, change isn't often immediate, but it is fast.

If you eat healthy, drink enough water, and exercise for a week, sure you're going to feel better almost immediately, but your health won't be completely changed after a week. However, if you consistently practice those things over the course of three months, six months, or even a year, your physical health will change drastically as a result of that consistency.

So if the change isn't happening immediately, don't get discouraged. Just stay consistent and give it time.

STRETCH YOURSELF

The second challenge I want to give you is to stretch yourself.

If you're KNOWING, GROWING, and GOING, and you have been giving it time and still don't see the change happening that you're desiring, it's time to stretch yourself, my friend.

Again, going back to the physical health metaphor, if you start eating healthier by eating at home rather than eating fast food, that might illicit some change initially. But after a while, you're going to need to stretch yourself more when it comes to your eating habits, like eating more fruits and vegetables or focusing on increasing your protein intake.

The same goes for working out. Maybe at first, you chose to prioritize movement by going on walks. And while that's a great step, you will get to a point where you need to stretch yourself further, maybe by running or lifting weights. We must continue to stretch ourselves if we want to continue to see progress.

It's no different for your spiritual life. You must continue to stretch yourself spiritually if you want to experience change.

Let's break down what stretching yourself looks like practically with KNOW, GROW, and GO.

STRETCH TO KNOW GOD BETTER

Marriages can get stale super quickly if you settle into the same pattern. If you go on a date with your spouse once a month, yes, that's good for your marriage. But if that's all you do, the relationship can start to feel stagnant. Sometimes you have to stretch yourself and try new things - whether that's serving your spouse in an unexpected way, planning a weekend getaway, or trying a new hobby together. New life is breathed into the marriage when you try new things.

The same is true when it comes to knowing God. Sometimes all you need to do is try something new to experience change. If you've never fasted before, try fasting. If you've never prayed out loud, try that. If you've never journaled your prayers, try writing them down. If you've never done a Bible reading plan, try that. Just try something new. This is what it looks like to stretch yourself when it comes to knowing God.

STRETCH TO GROW CLOSER TO OTHERS

If you're already in a small group, that's great! But are you stretching yourself within your small group?

There are three questions we ask everyone who is in a life group at our church. Are you there? Are you talking? And are you transparent?

In other words, when we ask, "Are you there?" we're asking if you are showing up consistently. Are you honoring the commitment you made to this group by making weekly attendance a priority? Or are you skipping group pretty often for reasons you could probably get out of?

When we ask, "Are you talking?" we're asking if you are contributing to group discussion. Are you answering questions? Are you sharing what God is teaching you lately? Or are you remaining quiet while others do the talking?

And when we ask, "Are you transparent?" we're asking if you are opening up and being vulnerable with the group. Are you letting the other group members in and telling them what's going on in your life? Are you confessing sin? Are you asking for accountability? Are you being honest with the group about your struggles?

So, with this in mind, let me ask you the same three questions.

When it comes to your small group, are you there? Are you talking? And are you transparent?

If you answered "not really" to any of those questions, that is the area I'd encourage you to stretch yourself in when it comes to GROWING.

STRETCH TO GO OUTSIDE YOUR COMFORT ZONE

When I first started working out, after about a week or so, I remember talking to my little brother who's a bodybuilder, and he asked me what I thought to be the strangest question. He said, "Did you feel the pump?"

Confused, I responded, "No...I did not feel the pump." My brother then proceeded to tell me that I needed to feel the pump - this feeling of your muscles filling with blood because you'd worked them so hard.

So I continued to work out, waiting to feel the pump, but it just wasn't happening. Finally, one day, I was so mad that I wasn't feeling the pump after my workouts that I put on some heavy metal music and pushed myself super hard in the gym. That led to me finally feeling the pump! Now I knew what my brother was talking about, but I had to push myself and stretch myself to get there.

This is what it looks like to stretch yourself as you GO and do things for God. Sometimes, the things we're doing for God are so easy and so painless that we never actually experience the power of God because we're not pushing ourselves or stepping out of our comfort zone.

We often say at our church that if you're handing out a bulletin on Sunday morning or giving people donuts at the cafe, that might not be enough to feel the pump of God's power as you serve. You might need to go one step further and stretch yourself as you serve in order to feel the pump.

As you think about how you're currently serving, is what you're doing for God giving you the chance to feel the pump of His power? Or are you doing things for God that are inside of your comfort zone?

If the latter is true, it might be time to stretch yourself as you GO.

OUR STORIES

There's one more thing I want to share with you before closing out this book.

I believe with every ounce of my being that KNOWING, GROWING, and GOING is the fastest way to change your life. I think I've made that pretty clear throughout this book. But I don't just believe that "because the Bible says so."

Yes, Jesus modeled for us exactly what it looks like to KNOW, GROW, and GO. He made it very clear that He will do an incredible work in your life if you do those three things. And that is more than enough of a reason to KNOW, GROW, and GO.

But I also want you to know that another reason I'm so passionate about encouraging and challenging people to KNOW, GROW, and GO is because of how I've seen God change my life when I do these three things. I'm not just passing along a message. I'm a living, breathing example of how God will change your life when you follow these three steps.

So to wrap up, I thought we (both Kristen and I) could share with you how we've lived out KNOWING, GROWING, and GOING in our own lives and how we've seen God bring change when we walked this journey with Him.

<u>VINCE</u>

For the last 15 years of following Jesus, I have been KNOWING, GROWING, and GOING. I have been meeting with mentors, groups of pastors, and my small group who I lean on, confess sin to, and share my life with. My goal is to spend time with God every day by reading my Bible and praying (even though it doesn't always happen every day). I've been trying to do things for God that stretch me, not just doing vocational ministry, but also doing things like getting together with my neighbors and inviting them to church.

This has been my spiritual growth strategy for the last decade and a half, and I really do feel like it's working. God has truly changed my life as I've chosen to KNOW, GROW, and GO, and I never want to get to a point where I'm not prioritizing these three things in my life.

<u>KRISTEN</u>

I accepted Jesus when I was five years old. Even though I had never heard the phrase "KNOW, GROW, and GO" until two years ago, I grew up learning the principles behind the phrase. I knew it was important to spend time with Jesus every day. I knew it was important to do life with other believers. And I knew it was important to use my God-given abilities to make a difference in the world around me.

But if I'm being honest, I haven't always been the best at doing all three of those consistently at the same time. There have been plenty of seasons where I've been KNOWING and GROWING, but not GOING, or I've been KNOWING and GOING, but not GROWING. You get the idea. And like we talked about before, I could see a bit of a change, but there were still areas of my life where I felt stuck.

On the other hand, when I look back over the last 26 years I've been following Jesus, in the seasons of my life where I *was* KNOWING, GROWING, and GOING all at the same time, those were the seasons where I saw God do some really big things in my life.

When I was simultaneously KNOWING, GROWING, and GOING, I found so much peace and purpose in the midst of a season of singleness I thought would never end. I experienced a whole new level of trust in Jesus when my life plan fell apart during my freshman year of college. I watched as God redeemed and restored my marriage that was barely hanging on by a thread. And that is just the tip of the iceberg.

This KNOW, GROW, and GO thing is the real deal. I can say that with so much confidence because I've seen firsthand how God brings change to a heart that is fully surrendered to Him, a heart that wants to KNOW Him, GROW together with other Christians, and GO make a difference for His Kingdom.

I know you want to experience that kind of change. That's why you picked up this book. And I want that change for you. But more importantly, God wants that change for you. And I can promise you that change will come if you KNOW, GROW, and GO.

Because at the end of the day, those three things really are the key to the fastest way to change your life.

The Good News:
How To Have A Relationship With Jesus

Have you ever wondered what life is really about or if there's something bigger out there? The Bible tells us that there is—a God who created us, loves us, and wants a personal relationship with us. That's where the Gospel comes in. "Gospel" simply means "good news," and it's the best news you'll ever hear. Let's talk about what it means to follow Jesus and how you can accept Him as your Savior today.

The Problem: Our Sin Separates Us from God

We were created to know God and live in close relationship with Him. But here's the problem: we've all messed up. The Bible says, *"For all have sinned and fall short of the glory of God"* (Romans 3:23). Sin is anything we do that goes against God's perfect standard. It's not just big mistakes—sin can be anything from lying to selfishness. Because God is holy and perfect, our sin separates us from Him. Romans 6:23 says, *"The wages of sin is death,"* which means that what we earn because of our sin is spiritual death—eternal separation from God.

The Solution: Jesus Came to Save Us

Here's the good news: God didn't leave us stuck in our sin. He loves us so much that He made a way for us to be forgiven. John 3:16 tells us, *"For God so loved the world that He gave His one and only Son, that whoever believes in Him shall not perish but have eternal life."* Jesus, God's Son, came to earth, lived a perfect life, and then died on the cross to take the punishment for our sins. He didn't stay dead—He rose from the grave three days later, defeating sin and death!

What We Need to Do: Trust in Jesus

So, how do we accept this incredible gift of forgiveness and eternal life? The Bible makes it clear: we need to believe in Jesus and what He did for us. Romans 10:9 says, *"If you declare with your mouth, 'Jesus is Lord,' and believe in your heart that God raised Him from the dead, you will be saved."* It's not about earning God's love through good deeds—salvation is a free gift from God. Ephesians 2:8-9 says, *"For it is by grace you have been saved, through faith—and this is not from yourselves, it is the gift of God—not by works, so that no one can boast."*

How You Can Respond

If you're ready to accept Jesus as your Savior and start a relationship with Him, it's as simple as believing and inviting Him into your life. Here's a prayer you can pray (but remember, it's not the exact words that matter—it's your heart behind them):

"Jesus, I know I've sinned and fallen short of Your perfect standard. I believe that You died on the cross to pay the price for my sins and rose again to give me eternal life. I ask You to forgive me, come into my life, and help me follow You from this day forward. Thank You for loving me and saving me. Amen."

What's Next?

If you just prayed that prayer and meant it, congratulations! You are now a child of God, and the Bible says all of heaven is celebrating with you (Luke 15:7). This is the beginning of a lifelong relationship with Jesus.

We hope that as you continue reading this book, you will gain helpful advice and learn practical next steps you can take as you pursue your new relationship with Jesus.

Remember, following Jesus isn't about being perfect—it's about growing in your relationship with Him and trusting Him to guide you each step of the way. Our goal is that this book is a tool that helps you do just that.

How To Spend Time With Jesus: A Daily Quiet Time Guide

Spending time with Jesus each day is one of the best ways to grow in your relationship with Him. It's not about checking a box, but about connecting with the One who loves you most. If you've ever wondered how to have a quiet time or how to make it meaningful, here are some practical tips to help you get started.

1. Find a Quiet Place

Choose a spot where you can be alone and free from distractions. It could be your bedroom, a cozy chair, or even a quiet corner of a coffee shop. Jesus often went to quiet places to pray (Luke 5:16), and it helps us focus on Him when we can get away from the noise of life.

2. Set Aside a Regular Time

Pick a time that works best for you—whether that's in the morning, during lunch, or at night. The Bible talks about meditating on God's Word "day and night" (Psalm 1:2), so the timing isn't as important as making it a habit. Start with 10-15 minutes a day and build from there.

3. Start with Prayer

Begin by talking to God. Thank Him for who He is and what He's done in your life. You can also ask Him to help you understand what you're about to read in the Bible. Philippians 4:6 reminds us, *"Do not be anxious about anything, but in every situation, by prayer and petition, with thanksgiving, present your requests to God."*

4. Read the Bible

The Bible is how God speaks to us, so spending time in Scripture is key. You can start by reading a chapter a day or following a Bible reading plan. Psalms and the Gospels (Matthew, Mark, Luke, and John) are great places to start. Psalm 119:105 says, *"Your word is a lamp for my feet, a light on my path."* As you read, think about what the passage is saying and how it applies to your life.

If you're looking to understand the Bible better as you read it, I wrote a step-by-step guide to the Bible that you can download for free by visiting thebridgenky.com/discover-the-bible.

5. Reflect and Journal

After reading, take a few minutes to reflect on what stood out to you. Ask yourself:

- What does this teach me about God?
- How can I apply this to my life today?

Writing down your thoughts or prayers in a journal can help you process and remember what God is teaching you. James 1:22 encourages us, *"Do not merely listen to the word, and so deceive yourselves. Do what it says."*

6. Spend Time in Worship

Worship isn't just for Sundays—it can be part of your daily quiet time! Listening to worship music can be a great addition to your daily time with God. Psalm 95:1-2 invites us, *"Come, let us sing for joy to the Lord; let us shout aloud to the Rock of our salvation."*

7. Be Still and Listen

Sometimes, it's easy to do all the talking, but God also wants us to be still and listen. After praying and reading, take a few moments to just sit in God's presence. Psalm 46:10 says, *"Be still, and know that I am God."* This is a great time to allow God to speak to your heart.

8. End with Gratitude

Wrap up your quiet time by thanking God for the time you've spent with Him. Gratitude shifts our focus to what God is doing in our lives, even in challenging seasons. 1 Thessalonians 5:18 reminds us, *"Give thanks in all circumstances; for this is God's will for you in Christ Jesus."*

Making It Personal

Remember, spending time with Jesus doesn't have to be perfect or follow a strict formula. It's about building a relationship. Some days, your quiet time might be longer; other days, it might be shorter. Some days you might implement every single tip listed above, and other days you might only implement a couple—and that's okay! The goal is to stay connected with Jesus and let Him guide you through each day.

Pro Tip: Set a reminder or an alarm on your phone to help make quiet time a regular part of your routine. And if you miss a day, don't be hard on yourself—just start fresh the next day!

Acknowledgments

Thank you to my wife, Joanna. I would have lost my sanity many times over if it were not for you. Thank you for holding me up in the countless moments you kept me from falling apart. I do not deserve you, but I am forever grateful. Thank you especially for being one of the early readers of this book, a mostly unglamorous job that you sacrificially did in the midst of the first few months of motherhood. There will be an extra "jewel in your crown" someday for that one!

Thank you to my daughter Lucy for filling our hearts with joy even in these first few weeks of life. I imagine that many kids do not want to read books that their parents write, but if you happen to crack this one open, know that your Mom and I love you very much. There is nothing we would love more than to have you be the first to see Aslan.

Thank you to the other advance editors/readers of this book, Brett Camp, Mariah Drohan, and Clay Knight. Thank you for being honest, especially when it was scary to say the helpful thing to your pastor. I hope we made it as easy as possible. You deserve to feel fulfilled when lives are impacted by this book. You are a part of that.

Thank you to the current board of elders at the Bridge: Gary Dawson, Randy Van Huss, Troy Guckiean, Pete Lewis, John Stark, and Tom Lange. It was a risk to greenlight this project so early in my tenure. Thanks for believing in me enough to let me give it a shot. I am grateful to be at the helm together with such godly men who are not just decision-makers, but fellow travelers on the journey of knowing, growing, and going.

Thank you to the Bridge staff leadership team at the time of this project: Chris Mitchell, Aaron Morgan, and Meredith Oesting. I have gotten far too much praise for decisions and insights that actually originated from you three. Thank you for thinking clearly when I couldn't, and for moving us toward the right and hard decisions even when I was the one pushing back.

Maybe most deservedly, thank you to Kristen Cave, who was really far more than a contributing writer. This book would not exist if you had not been willing to go on the journey. You more accurately deserve the title of co-writer. I am probably not disciplined or focused enough to ever write a book on my own. In many of the chapters, you contributed some of the major metaphors and examples. If this book is helpful to anyone, they should know that it is both of our voices they are hearing clearly. Thank you, Kristen. I hope this is the first of more to come, both working together and the books you will write on your own journey!

Lastly, thank you to the people of The Bridge Church. You have had to suffer through the great trial of attending a church led by a pastor in his first five years of experience. Thank you for having grace for me, for all the ways I know I've fallen short and all the ways I don't. Thank you also for inviting your friends, for baptizing them, for going to life group even when it was hard, and for serving on teams even when it meant waking up early. Thank you for loving Jesus and letting Him change your life. I truly believe that this is just the beginning.

About the Authors

Vince Pierri

Vince holds a bachelor's degree in English from Northeastern Illinois University and a Master of Divinity from Trinity Evangelical Divinity School. He is married to Joanna Pierri, and together they have a daughter named Lucy.

Vince is passionate about preaching, leadership, strategy, and coaching other communicators. He serves as the lead pastor of The Bridge Church in Alexandria, Kentucky, a vibrant and growing community in the Cincinnati, Ohio suburbs. The Bridge's thriving ministry model is built on the principles described in this book.

Kristen Cave

Kristen earned her Bachelor of Science in Communication from Kennesaw State University. She is a writer, podcaster, and youth pastor's wife, currently serving alongside her husband, Kevin, at The Bridge Church in Alexandria, Kentucky.

Kristen loves helping others find and follow Jesus, and she is passionate about sharing her experiences and faith through her writing and podcast. When she's not serving in ministry or working on her next project, you can find her spending time with her husband and two dogs, Sparky and Sadie.

Made in the USA
Middletown, DE
13 February 2025